LIVING
BEYOND
YOURSELF

HOW INDIA BROKE MY HEART FOR
THE GREAT COMMISSION

TODD VANEK

Mission India
PO Box 141312
Grand Rapids, MI 49514-1312
(877) 644-6342
info@missionindia.org
www.missionindia.org

LIVING BEYOND YOURSELF
© 2020 Todd VanEk
Published by Mission India

ISBN 978-0-9788551-8-5

First printing, 2020

1 2 3 4 5 6 7 Printing/Year 25 24 23 22 21 20

Design by Caleb Hannah

Edited by Jim and Sue Holmes

Library of Congress Cataloging-in-Publication Data

Library of Congress Control Number: 2020920544

In loving memory of Dr. John F. DeVries

1936 – 2020

In the pages that follow, you will often hear me reference a dear friend and mentor of mine, John DeVries. The impact that John has had on my life and ministry is unmeasurable. In fact, even though he didn't write any of the words that follow, he inspired nearly all of them.

John went home to Glory just as this book was headed off to the printer. I dedicate this book to him.

John founded Mission India, the organization I now serve (as its third president), in 1978. And for the rest of his life, John remained devoted to seeing people in India come to know and receive the love of Jesus. The seed of that devotion was planted in the early 1970s, when John visited India for the first time.

He arrived in India and was immediately overwhelmed by the smells, heat, blaring horns, crowds of people, and spiritual darkness. John summarized that trip by saying, "India is an assault on the senses." He wanted none of it and immediately started praying his "Jonah prayer" – *Lord, I'll serve you anywhere but here*. Call me anywhere you want, but never India.

As much as he wanted to ignore it, John felt a calling from God to serve this different and distant land on the other side of the globe and John answered that call. And even though it was a place that intimidated him, confused him, and frustrated him, it also broke his heart for the things of God.

As I think about that calling and how John responded, I sometimes wonder: Would I have had the faith to move forward back then?

Jesus tells us in Matthew 17:20, "…if you have faith as small as a mustard seed, you can say to this mountain, 'Move from here to there,' and it will move. Nothing will be impossible for you." John's legacy is his faith and obedience to God's call – *he lived beyond himself* – and I pray that you and I can lead and live with the same passionate faith and obedience that John displayed throughout his life.

On behalf of the tens of millions of once-unreached people in India whose lives have now been transformed by the love of Christ, thank you, John. Thank you for your legacy from day one until now. Thank you for allowing all of us who are part of Mission India to witness the truth of Ephesians 3:20, that God is "able to do immeasurably more than all we ask or imagine, according to his power that is at work within us."

Todd VanEk
November 11, 2020

Table of Contents

INTRODUCTION:
Learning to Live Beyond Yourself

The first nudge happened in 2004 when Dr. John DeVries, a frequent visitor to the Michigan church I was pastoring, approached me after a morning worship service. John was a well-known and extremely gifted preacher, and so I felt really complimented to hear him say, "Todd, that was a great sermon you preached this morning." He then grabbed my arm, looked me straight in the eye, and said, "You need to go to India. I have arranged to cover your airfare and expenses to join me on my trip there next January."

If you knew John, you might have known that that was the most expensive "free" trip I had ever been offered. I had never thought about India. It wasn't on my radar. I was an extremely busy pastor of a fast-growing congregation, and it was hard to imagine taking two weeks off to travel to the other side of the world. What would be the payoff? And, anyway, what did India matter to me or to my congregation? We were all so invested in our own people, our own community, and our own lives — we could hardly think about something so far away.

Somehow, the Holy Spirit prompted me to accept John's

invitation. That trip in January 2005 dramatically changed my life. All my experiences shared in this book grew out of that first connection to India. It should not be this way, but sometimes it takes a trip to the other side of the world to shake us out of our lethargy, to cause us to begin to see the world as God sees it, to get beyond ourselves.

Subsequent to that first trip to India, God nudged me and my family to do something that forever changed the way we see the world. One day I came home, and my wife, Jean, said, "I need to talk to you. You better sit down." I sat down. Then Jean said, "I think God is calling us to adopt and I want to know what you think about this."

You have to understand that we already had four beautiful children — two of them were fully grown and out of the house — and we were not getting any younger. So, I said, "I don't think so..." Jean replied, "Will you pray about it?" I said yes, and that's how I lost that argument!

At the time, I was in the middle of a sermon series on the book of James. It just so happened that the very next Sunday I was preaching on the text from James 1:27, which reads: "Religion that God our Father accepts as pure and faultless is this: to look after orphans and widows in their distress and to keep oneself from being polluted by the world." Have you ever heard that pastors often preach to themselves? Well, in that case, it was literally true. And thank God I listened!

Because of our relationship with Mission India, we decided that India was the only country we would consider adopting from. That is how our youngest daughter, Jori, came to be a part of our forever family. Jean and I shared the experience of how we came to be gifted with Jori in a blog we published several years ago. Here is what we shared:

"We would like to begin by giving thanks to the Lord God Almighty, first of all, for this entire journey which we began in the late summer of 2008. He has proven Himself to be faithful time and time again!!! After much prayer and many discussions with other families that had adopted internationally, we decided to proceed with adopting a child from India.

"Our connection to India began with a ministry called Mission India. Todd had traveled to India and witnessed the terrible plight of little girls. We felt called to adopt a child from India and we began our process in October 2008. God took our family down the path of trusting in Him, and, once again, His sovereignty in our lives has blown us away! After 2 ½ years of preparation, home studies, and much prayer, in November of 2011, God connected us with our baby girl!!!

"Our first glimpse of Jori (Manjari is her Indian name) was a six-month-old picture of a beautiful, darling, eyes-bigger-than-life bundle wrapped snuggly in a baby blanket. At this moment in time, Jori was fifteen months old. We completed the large amounts of paperwork and sent our dossier to India. Due to

our family moves to California and then back to Michigan, we had to undergo four home studies, the final one coming after Jori had already been identified as our potential daughter. And then we waited ... and waited some more.... Our journey has been filled with very high "ups" and very low "downs." We were rejected by CARA (India's Governmental Agency for International Adoptions). We appealed their decision and were rejected again. We appealed a second time and, finally, were approved! Throughout this entire time, we have questioned, struggled with God, and begged for His mercy to be shown to our family and to the beautiful little girl that we had grown to love with all our hearts!

"We believe wholeheartedly that the sole reason that we have been blessed to be Jori's forever family has been for God's glory to be displayed through the power of prayer! God also blessed our older children throughout this journey: Ashley, Luke, Nolan, and Madison's encouragement, faith, understanding, excitement, and love have been a bright spot in the good times and bad times of our journey. Jori has the most amazing siblings to love, learn from, cry with, laugh with, fight with, and just live life with!

"And, finally, we are so thankful for the many prayer warriors that have brought our family before Jesus Christ's throne over and over again, for their faithfulness to us! So, it was with this whole 'thankful' theme that God designed for Todd, Jean, Nolan, and Madi that we got on a plane and set out to bring our daughter home on Thanksgiving Day! Do we not serve a mighty God?!?!?!

"Isaiah 30:18 says, 'Yet the LORD longs to be gracious to you; therefore he will rise up to show you compassion. For the LORD is a God of justice. Blessed are all who wait for Him!'"

In Jori, God has sent a precious piece of India into the heart of our family. And, in doing that, God is showing us every single day how much He loves the people of India, and how much He longs for each of us to reflect that love in whatever way we can. That means personal transformation and an explosion of joy in our family. It would be that joy that would empower me to say yes to the next encounter that God orchestrated in my life.

I was serving a church of 2,500 in Holland, Michigan when Dave Stravers, former president of Mission India, called me and asked if I would meet him for lunch. I thought he wanted to have lunch with me because he was going to ask me if our church could give Mission India more money. So, I went to lunch with arms folded, waiting for him to get to "the ask." Finally, Dave said, "Todd, there is something I need to ask you" and I thought, "Here it comes...."

"Would you consider being the next president of Mission India?"

You could have knocked me over with a feather. Some kids grow up and dream of being doctors or firemen or lawyers or truck drivers or crane operators. But, ever since I entered the ministry, I have dreamed of being a part of an organization that has laser focus on living out the Great Commission. As I look back, I see how twenty years ago it was God inviting me to India, and it was God giving us Jori, and it was God preparing me and Jean to give the rest of our lives to God's plan to reach India for Christ.

In His sovereign control of our lives, God knew that, prior to bringing Jori home, He had to get me to India and get our family involved with Mission India, and, prior to my becoming president of Mission India, He had to give me a personal connection to the lost people of India. I have a debt of love to India and I am humbled to reflect on the ways God has shaped my entire life to bring me to this joy-filled excitement of getting my life in tune with His vision.

The rest of this book is my attempt to share that joy with you and all it could mean for your own fulfillment as a follower of Christ. Much of what you will read is about India. Why India? Many reasons will become apparent. But, first and foremost among them, I believe India is the very best place in the world to live beyond yourself. It's more beyond yourself — and more in line with God's will — than anywhere else on earth.

CHAPTER 1:
Crying God's Tears

I grew up a closet charismatic. Every Sunday morning, my family attended a traditional church with formal Presbyterian-style worship services; and many Sunday nights, we would go to a Pentecostal church. When I was ten years old, the minister at the Pentecostal church gave a call to receive Christ and hundreds of people started walking down the aisle. I asked my mom, "What are all those people doing?" She said, "Giving their life to Christ." I asked, "All of them?" I just couldn't believe that this many people didn't already know Jesus.

I remember another time when I was in middle school and my parents served as volunteers and donors of a Christ-centered recovery ministry. As a middle school student, I remember going to multiple graduation nights where two hundred people would graduate from their program and a handful of them would give their testimony. They would talk about how their lives had been delivered from drugs, alcohol, or prostitution. I was amazed by how Jesus could bring such radical change to people who were so far away from God.

It was in high school that my pastor invited me to join the

evangelism team. We would follow up with people who visited our church and share the Gospel with them. Again, I was shocked to discover how many people did not know Jesus — and all the more shocked that people were praying in their living rooms and around their kitchen tables to begin a relationship with Jesus. At seventeen years of age, I began to understand that the Gospel is a living, breathing, moving Gospel that is seen in its ability to produce fruit by transforming people's lives. We are to proclaim a living Jesus who enters lives and transforms people. This is completely different than proclaiming that Jesus came to die strictly so we can go to Heaven. It's so much more!

Nearly twenty years later, I took my first trip to India, a country where 1.3 billion people don't know Jesus (according to the 2011 India Census). Of the total population, 85 percent of them — Hindus and Muslims — don't even know a single Christian, and 400 million of them have never heard the name "Jesus." For the first time in my life, I met people who were unreached by the Gospel — that is, they had no access to Scripture, other believers, Bibles, Christian literature, or Christian broadcast, and it brought me to tears. It became so clear to me that the world is an unimaginably big place and millions of people in the world have never had the opportunity to meet Christ, to experience the single most important transformational event that can come to any human being. More of those people live in India than anywhere else.

It hit me in January 2005. I was in India to see firsthand what the

Holy Spirit was doing there. It was a mind-blowing experience. But it was the Sunday morning service that made the greatest impact on me where, as the honored, American guest, I was invited to give the message. I was not really prepared, especially not prepared to preach with a translator. I nervously delivered the worst sermon I have ever given. I was so embarrassed. At the end of the message, I invited anyone present to make a decision to follow Jesus. People leaped out of their chairs in response to my simple invitation. So many people responded with passion and tears. I've never had such a response to a sermon, not even the best sermon I have ever preached!

For me, this was a critical, life-changing event. I realized that the Holy Spirit was doing something so powerful to reach the unreached people of India, and doing that in ways that I had never experienced before. I decided that instant that I would do everything I could to join the Spirit in His work. I was seeing the world beyond my context. As a result, I started to live life differently. My wife, Jean, and I started to think more globally; we started to give differently; we started to pray differently; and we started to think about things concerning which, previously, we had never given a thought. We shed tears for the lost and for those for whom Jesus died, for those who do not know of His great sacrifice for them.

To this day, God continues to drive this truth deep into my heart in multiple ways. One night, as I was walking my dog, I was listening to a message by David Platt, who, at the time, was president of the International Mission Board, the largest mission-sending organization in the world. He was preaching on Romans 1:14-16a: "I am under a debt both to Greeks and to barbarians, both to the wise and to the foolish. So, I am eager to preach the gospel to you also who are in Rome. For I am not ashamed of the gospel, for it is the power of God for salvation to everyone who believes" (paraphrased).

I was so impacted by this text and the idea of being in debt that I read it over and over again, thinking this was strange talk from Paul. Platt shares, "Usually, we get into debt because someone has loaned us something. The Greeks and the barbarians have not loaned Paul anything. Paul has never even met them. Yet, Paul says that he is deeply indebted to them, to the point of giving his own life in order to pay this debt."

As I reflected on this, I thought how interesting it is that this debt is not to his parents, to his church, or to his mission agency. The verse states that the debt is not to God. Paul makes it crystal clear elsewhere in the book of Romans that God has freely given him his inheritance in the Kingdom. That is the meaning of grace. We have all received this free gift of grace and we don't become debtors to God because of it. You cannot pay God back for His grace in your life. Otherwise, grace would no longer be grace — a free gift.

The best thing about grace is that it pays debts. Grace forgives our debts. So, what is this debt of love to the Greeks and the non-Greeks, the wise and foolish? It is a debt of love. It's the gift of grace that must propel us to live beyond ourselves so that sharing God's grace with others is the most important priority of our life, because to know the Gospel is about proclaiming and demonstrating the power of the Gospel.

Our Heavenly Father has given us the incredible riches of the knowledge of the Good News of Jesus, who came to earth to die and rise again, and who invites all people everywhere to enter His Kingdom. This Good News of deliverance from sin, from evil, and from death is meant to be shared with everyone, everywhere. Those of us who possess these riches have an obligation to share them with those who do not yet possess them. Paul is saying if you receive God's grace, you must *proclaim* God's grace. That is what drove Paul.

Paul is writing this letter to the church at Rome because he wants to take the Gospel to Spain, to people who have never heard the Gospel. The whole book was written for that purpose: to encourage the church to join this task of taking the Gospel to those who had never heard it. Romans was not written with the purpose of creating a great theological treatise on our faith, even though it is that. Rather, Paul was finding it difficult to drum up support for his proposed mission to Spain. We can only imagine the reaction Paul would receive to his calling to Spain: "Why go to Spain? We don't know anyone there!" "They live on the edge of the world. They are uncivilized pagans." "Why can't we just keep helping the churches in Italy, Macedonia, and Asia? They have needs, too."

Paul's answer to these objections is that we have a debt of love, a debt of grace, and we need to pay this debt by sharing the Good News with the people of Spain who have never heard about Jesus.

This is why the book of Romans describes a love of God that overflows, that is more than you can handle, an excess of God's mercy, not only to Jews but to everyone. That is why Jesus told Paul that He was sending him to share this love with others. The extravagant inventory of love that God has deposited into our account needs to be freely distributed among all of those people whom God is targeting but who have not yet received it.

For reasons known only to God, He has decided that the only way people will receive the gift of eternal life is through His human children. God is not going to send His angels to share the Gospel with the Spaniards or with anyone else who is waiting to hear it. Those of us who have heard the Gospel must share the message, particularly with those unreached by the Gospel. It is the debt of love that every believer has.

That obligation is huge. Today, there are about seven billion people in the world and two billion of them are unreached. Put yourself in the shoes of one of these two billion people in the world. I am not talking about being lost. There is a difference between being lost and being unreached. Many people have heard about Jesus and have ignored or rejected what they have heard. They are lost. But if you are unreached, you likely don't even know Jesus exists. Platt expresses it this way:

> You have no access to a Bible, a believer, or a church. Maybe you're living in Nigeria or Cameroon and you practice voodoo in your attempts to appease and direct the evil spirits around you. Maybe you're in India, and you offer incense and food and prayers every day to gods you've crafted with your own hands. Maybe you're in Saudi Arabia and you bow down five times a day to recite rote prayers to a god who is so remote and far away. Maybe you're in the mountains of Tibet where you worship the Buddha, and you've sent your firstborn son off to the monastery to attain Buddhahood. Or maybe you're in China or North Korea and you've rejected the idea of God altogether. You hardly have a concept of God.

If you are in one of these situations, and unless something changes, you will likely be born, live, and die without ever hearing the Gospel, the Good News of what God has done in Christ. And the odds are very high that you live in India.

Indians make up one-sixth of the world's population. With a birth rate that adds 41,000 souls every day, India will soon become the world's most populous country. The vast majority of them only know hopelessness in the face of poverty and injustice, living lives of anxiety, fear, and meaninglessness. This manifests itself in things like: child slavery, child brides, infanticide, malnutrition, sex trafficking, corruption, oppression of women, ethnic violence, illiteracy, and the caste system.

India is also the center of idol worship in our world — a place where people worship literally hundreds of millions of gods and goddesses. Do you think the connection between this level of hopelessness and this level of idolatry is coincidence?

Consider what it must be like for Christ in His exalted state, who when He was on earth wept in pity over the lost people of Jerusalem, that 1.3 billion image-bearers of God should be subject to such tortures of Satan without any knowledge of the salvation that He offers to them! Instead, 900 million Hindus seek deliverance from 330 million gods, and more than 175 million Muslims perform the self-denial duties of Islam with the uncertain hope of their own version of paradise. Each year, millions die without ever knowing Christ. They die without hope simply because no one has told them that, in Christ, the final sacrifice has already been offered on their behalf.

Their lives do not have to end this way. It does not have to be this way. We should all dream of the day when all people will have the opportunity to hear, to understand, and to make the decision of whether or not to receive His free gift. So, we cry God's tears for the lost. We also dream God's dreams for those who are no longer lost. Ultimately, we will all have to live beyond ourselves because, like Paul, we all have a debt of love to reach those unreached by God's love!

This is not something we should enter into lightly. Recently, I received an email from a colleague who shared:

> Today, I'm praying and fasting for God to give me His love (not my human, limited love, but His), specifically for the nation of India. I need a "dislocated heart" for His people there. When I asked this, I believe God told me that His love toward India was deep, intense, and very painful. And then He asked me if I *really* wanted it. Gulp! I know I can't do this job and pray for India unless I have God's broken heart for them. So do I want the *pain* of His love for India? No! But then, again, yes, I do! It is absolutely necessary.

> I am waiting on Him for this and when it comes, I believe I will get to know God better by being privy to His longing over them and His lonely, one-sided desire for them to know Him and return His love. And in gaining His love, I believe God is hinting at the possibility that it would also set me free from more of my selfishness, entitlement, as well as trivial, useless things in my life.

Now, it is one thing to ask for a dislocated heart for myself regarding the people of India, but I am also asking that God gives it to all of us (even more than we have right now)! May God's aggressive love for India begin as a massive movement within us: you, me, the board, staff, donors, families, churches, other states, and even other countries! All over the world! God alone can do this. He alone can get us there. But, oh, to be a person that God would entrust His heart to … that is my desire.

If you want to live beyond yourself, you need to cry God's tears. God has passionate, heartfelt concern for lost people. Without this concern for others, no one can live beyond themselves. The tears of God Himself are the best guide and surest motivation to encourage our alignment with His priorities.

Questions for discussion:

1. What struck you most about this chapter?

2. Share a time in your life when God gave you a passionate and heartfelt concern for someone else.

3. God forms us and shapes us over our lifetime to live beyond ourselves. In what ways has God been shaping you to live beyond yourself?

4. Read again Romans 1:14-16. In your opinion, how do

these verses relate to living beyond ourselves?

5. When you think of living beyond yourself, do you tend to think about this mostly in a local context (concerning people you see face to face) or a global context (concerning people who might live far away)? Why?

6. In your opinion, how can we best help ourselves and others catch a vision and hear God's call to live for His global glory?

Optional exercise: Pray together in a group, asking God to give you a passion and heartfelt concern for others so that you can start living beyond yourselves.

CHAPTER 2:
Who is Sovereign in Your Life?

We live in a world that is continually calling us to give our allegiance to a host of realities that stand over and against God. The biblical word for this is "idolatry." Although idolatry is a reality everywhere in our world, India is a dramatic case study in the malicious power of idolatry.

Of India's vast population, 74 percent follow some form of what we call "Hinduism." For most of them, this means worshipping multiple gods, usually represented by sacred images in their temples, businesses, or homes. Many Hindus claim that there are 330 million of these gods or goddesses. Although, of course, I've never seen them listed in any one place! But I have seen thousands and thousands of people in India bowing down to idols made with human hands, believing these deities might give them what they desire.

So, there is Ganesh, the elephant-headed god of good fortune. Lakshmi is the benevolent goddess of wealth. Then there is Hanuman, the "monkey god," who is the patron of the martial arts, meditation, and diligent scholarship. Shiva, "the destroyer," is often depicted with a serpent around his neck.

The other "destroyer of evil" and "protector goddess" is Kali, usually depicted with a necklace of skulls, four arms holding a sword, one or more severed heads, and a bowl to catch the blood dripping from the head.

To be fair, many Hindu deities are not weapon-wielding, fire-breathing, bloodthirsty creatures. Many deities represent good things. However, every last one calls its worshippers to honor something other than God as the supreme value in life. When I am in India, I cannot escape the role that fear plays in the worship of these idols. That should make sense to those of us who are familiar with Exodus 32, which tells the story of the seductive influence of idols in the lives of God's people. The people could not stay focused on the one true God, and it was because of their fear.

"When the people saw that Moses was so long in coming down from the mountain, they gathered around Aaron and said, 'Come, make us gods who will go before us. As for this fellow Moses who brought us up out of Egypt, we don't know what has happened to him'" (v. 1). They were afraid Moses and God had forgotten about them, so Aaron gives in to their fear. The passage goes on to say, "Aaron answered them, 'Take off the gold earrings that your wives, your sons and your daughters are wearing, and bring them to me.' So all the people took off their earrings and brought them to Aaron. He took what they handed him and made it into an idol cast in the shape of a calf, fashioning it with a tool. Then they said, 'These are your gods, Israel, who brought you up out of Egypt'" (Exodus 32:2-4).

Meanwhile, up on the mountain, God informs Moses of what has happened in verses 9 and 10: "'I have seen these people,' the Lord said to Moses, 'and they are a stiff-necked people. Now leave me alone so that my anger may burn against them and that I may destroy them. Then I will make you into a great nation.'"

This story reminds us that we all have a temptation to idolatry. It was not the heathens that began to worship the golden calf, but God's own people, the same people who had witnessed His mighty miracles of deliverance out of Egyptian slavery. For some reason, God's people become afraid and lose sight of the one true God and the truth that He is a good God, full of grace.

Moses was gone for forty days and nights, and all the people had to do was wait. Just wait. They were not hungry. They were not thirsty. They were not in danger. All they had to do was wait for Moses to return, just trust God enough to wait. They didn't want to wait. They couldn't accept God's timing and their anxiety drove them away from God as they told themselves story after story.

Have you ever had times in your life when you felt that God was no longer present, that there was something not right in your life that needed fixing and the waiting was burdening you? Have you ever felt that no matter how hard you have reached out for God, you couldn't find Him? When those times come, what is it that you do? Where is it that you go? If it's not to God Himself, but to anything else, no matter how good, no matter how appealing, then you've just surrendered to idolatry.

In India, people turn to idols because they have no alternative. Most of them know nothing whatsoever about the one true Creator God, the Savior God, the God of love and power. He's been up on the mountain, out of sight and out of mind, for centuries. As a result, so many Indian lives overflow with spiritual darkness and suffering. Their example warns us against the dangers of substituting something else for the one true God. However, in India, idols are easy to see and identify; they are tangible images made of stone and wood with people bowing down to them. But, for us, it's different. We're good at hiding our idols.

Thankfully, the Exodus story and the Hindu experience can help us understand what makes an idol.

First of all, an idol always reflects the culture in which people live. The Israelites turned their attention immediately to what they knew: the Baals of Canaan. These were the gods who, according to the beliefs of the Canaanites, brought rain to their crops; the gods who protected them from their enemies; the gods who guaranteed material prosperity. One of the oldest of these gods is Baal, which is represented by a bull. It's no accident that when you are in India, you will encounter this deity in multiple places.

The Israelites could also have chosen, and later did choose, other familiar gods: Ashtoreth, the goddess of fertility; Molech, the god who answers prayers in response to child sacrifice; or Dagon, the god who blesses fishermen and farmers. Many Indians choose gods that appeal to them or frighten them. What gods do Westerners choose? How about Maserati, the god of speed? Or Remington, the god of home security? Or Benjamin Franklin, the god of financial security?

Our modern-day idols also reflect the cultures in which we live, those possessions and powers that are familiar to us, that promise to make us happy, meet our wants and needs, and enrich our lives. Our idols are considered normal, understandable, and acceptable.

A second way to identify an idol is to realize that, no matter how much one gives, an idol never brings true, lasting satisfaction. The Israelites collected their most valuable jewelry to construct their idol. They built an altar to it. They conducted a festival around it. They sang and danced themselves to exhaustion around it. They devoted their physical, mental, and financial energies to it. Later on in their history, they even sacrificed their children to their idols.

Whether I live in India or America, the primary demand that I will make of an idol is that it serve me, work for me, perform for me, produce for me. But, as a consequence, I will end up serving, working, and performing for my idol. Whether my ultimate goal is success in school, a well-decorated house, an enviable vehicle, a successful career, or perfect children, I will be tempted to invest massive amounts of time and money to forsake all boundaries, to justify a consuming passion for that which drives me. Eventually, our idols take more and more, and give less and less. No idol ever says, "Come to me, all you who are weary and burdened, and I will give you rest" (Matthew 11:28).

Why did Moses grind up the golden calf, put it in Israel's water, and make them drink it? Perhaps he was telling them, "You think this satisfies your hunger the way God satisfies it? Will it give you energy and power? All right, drink it up and tell me how you feel."

I've noticed something that happens in India when people who have worshipped idols their whole life suddenly discover the Good News of Jesus Christ. Before their transformation, there is an idol in every corner of their house. Very soon after starting to follow Jesus, those images just disappear. Why would they want a reminder of the empty promises and burdensome demands of their idols when they have met the Master of the universe and the Savior of all who trust in Him? For the first time in their life, they can live without fear. They can live beyond themselves.

As believers, some of us have forgotten the freedom we have

received in Christ. For us, the temptation is to rationalize our idolatry. That is exactly what Aaron did when he said to Moses, "Don't let your anger burn against me. You know the people. They're bent on evil. They made me do it, Moses. I didn't want to do it." And then he explained in an almost comically unbelievable lie, "I took the gold and threw it into the fire and, wow, out came this calf!"

I think my ten-year-old daughter could have come up with a better story than that. But it only illustrates what we have all experienced: We often desperately rationalize why that thing that we worship is not really an idol. That is what Aaron was doing. He was rationalizing. The people of Israel wanted to get to the Promised Land, and Moses had been gone so long that they were not getting any closer. That's when they reasoned that they should make another god.

What the Lord had really called them to do was become a light to the nations. They were called to demonstrate the true worship of the one true God, to become an attractive alternative to the idolatry all around them. Just a short time earlier, God had made this clear to Moses: "'You yourselves have seen what I did to Egypt, and how I carried you on eagles' wings and brought you to myself. Now if you obey me fully and keep my covenant, then out of all nations you will be my treasured possession. Although the whole earth is mine, you will be for me a kingdom of priests and a holy nation.' These are the words you are to speak to the Israelites" (Exodus 19:4-6).

God is indescribably good. Everything that we know about goodness and the demand for justice and the longing for the world to be right, it all comes from this God. He made Israel to be in a loving relationship with Him, to model who He is to all the nations, to see how very different He is from the gods of the nations.

So, you have statements from the prophets, like Micah 6:6-7, which says, "With what shall I come before the Lord … with burnt offerings … with thousands of rams…? Shall I offer my firstborn…?" (Human sacrifice … that's what people did to the gods to get out of them what they wanted from them.) "And what does the Lord require of you? To act justly and to love mercy and to walk humbly with your God" (Micah 6:8).

This is unprecedented. This is what made the small, insignificant nation of Israel the most powerful, spiritual force in the Old Testament universe. It changed the world. Because of this "one-God" alternative to idolatry, this weak, poor, little country changed everything.

It is easy to read the story in Exodus 32 and think "Oh, those silly Israelites, making earrings into idols." But in Nehemiah, the Psalms, and 1 Corinthians, the writers of Scripture come back to that story again and again and remind those of us who follow Christ that we, too, are in danger of idolatry. The cost of idolatry is always more serious than we first suppose. I am sure Aaron did not think through the full impact of his decision: In the end,

33

three thousand people lost their lives, God's judgment was poured out, and Israel's witness to other nations was destroyed.

If I realize the true price tag for idolatry, I'm less likely to give in to it. In the words of Tim Keller, "Why does God hate idolatry so much? Well, it's not just because of what idolatry does to God; although, of course, it robs Him of the honor and worship and adoration that He deserves, but God hates it because of what it does to us because it train wrecks life."[1]

Thank God for a man like Moses who lived so far beyond himself that he offered his own life to protect his idolatrous people! Moses' finest hour was not leading the Exodus, splitting the sea, or receiving the Ten Commandments. Moses' greatest, most glorious moment on earth was when he stood before God, pleading for his people, fighting for forgiveness. He said, "But now, please forgive their sin — but if not, then blot me out of the book you have written" (Exodus 32:32). God was so pleased with Moses for living beyond himself that He agreed to Moses' request, and Israel was saved from extinction because Moses knew that God alone was sovereign and that He alone was worthy of their worship and praise. He pleads for God to forgive Israel so they can be who God called them to be: A nation that lives beyond fear of abandonment, waiting and believing in God's promises, declaring these promises, and demonstrating their belief by faithfully waiting and believing.

If you want to live beyond yourself, you must acknowledge the sovereignty of God in your life. Only by the power and authority of God will you be able to live beyond yourself.

Questions for discussion:

1. What struck you most about this chapter? Was there anything in this chapter that you disagreed with or found difficult to accept?

2. Read again Exodus 32:1-6 and Exodus 32:31-32. In your opinion, what was the main sin of Israel in this story? Are there any similar ways that we are tempted to sin today?

3. In what ways does the world around us try to challenge the sovereignty of the one true God?

4. List some ways that you can keep focused every day on the one true God, even in the midst of our idol-centric culture.

CHAPTER 3:
The Sovereignty of God

You can live beyond yourself while overcoming anxiety or fear because God is in control. He will call us to step out of our comfort zones in order to understand and build our lives on the power and authority of who He is.

I have always been in awe of the sovereignty of God. Since I began working at Mission India, I have come to understand this characteristic of God more fully and personally than ever before in my life. This has given me tremendous confidence as well as a lens to help me keep focus as I walk through times of anxiety and fear. The sovereignty of God presents us with two pillars that help us deal with the anxiety of life. First, God is sovereign because He is all-powerful — He has the power, strength, and might to rule. Second, God is sovereign because He has all authority — His power is not arbitrary; He has the "right" to rule. These pillars are firmly established on His unconditional love.

Isaiah, the great prophet of God's power and authority, wrote:

> The people walking in darkness have seen a great light; on those living in the land of deep darkness a light has

dawned. You have enlarged the nation and increased their joy; they rejoice before you…. For to us a child is born, to us a son is given, and the government will be on his shoulders. And he will be called Wonderful Counselor, Mighty God, Everlasting Father, Prince of Peace. Of the greatness of his government and peace there will be no end (Isaiah 9:2, 3, 6-7).

These words come on the tail of Isaiah 6 where the prophet has a vision and proclaims: "In the year that King Uzziah died, I saw the Lord, high and exalted, seated on a throne; and the train of his robe filled the temple" (v.1). The throne of God is not one among many thrones; it is high, and it is lifted up as the only source of power and authority. Isaiah sees no other thrones.

In his book, *All Authority: How the Authority of Christ Upholds the Great Commission*, Joey Shaw writes:

> The supreme authority of Jesus is the biblical foundation for local and global mission. Consider "The Great Commission" in Matthew 28:18-20. First, in verse 18, Jesus declares his supreme authority over all, "All authority has been given to me in heaven and on earth." *Then*, Jesus gives the famous mandate (vv. 19-20): "Go, therefore, and make disciples of all nations, baptizing them in the name of the Father and of the Son and of the Holy Spirit, teaching them to observe everything I have commanded you." It is no coincidence that the doctrinal declaration of Matthew 28:18 precedes

the mandate of Matthew 28:19; for the authority of verse 18 is linked with the power needed to fulfill the mandate in verse 19. Trust is the bedrock of mission.[2]

This is good news for Isaiah and good news for us. I was at a missions conference some time ago and the speaker was talking about the sovereignty of God, which he explained this way: For us, it means Iran's leader, Hassan Rouhani, is not sovereign because God is sovereign over all; North Korea's leader, Kim Jong-un, is not sovereign because God is sovereign over all; Russia's leader, Vladimir Putin, is not sovereign because God is sovereign over all; Syria's leader, Bashar al-Assad, is not sovereign because God is sovereign over all; India's leader, Narendra Modi, is not sovereign because God is sovereign over all.

God is sovereign over every single person and nation. This means that He has the right to rule and the power to rule. He is sovereign over you and me — our lives, our goals, and our actions. But here is the main thing it means for those of us who want to live beyond ourselves: God's number one purpose in this world is that those in darkness would recognize His sovereignty. Those in deep darkness must come to know this Wonderful Counselor, this Mighty God, this Everlasting Father, this Prince of Peace.

That is God's sovereign will for this world and His sovereign purposes work toward that reality. We must think about God's sovereignty with an understanding of His desire to reach those who have never heard this Good News.

God's sovereignty informs us of His purpose in creating the world, sending His Son, redeeming all of creation, orchestrating and ruling our lives so that people come to know His amazing and powerful grace.

It surprises and upsets some people to hear that God's sovereign rule is "good news." Many people reject the rule of God. How can an all-powerful God who commands obedience and judges sinners be good news for me when I want to do things my way without interference from an Almighty? But it is good news! It's the best news we could hear. What people are misunderstanding is the connection between God's authority and power grounded in His love. This is what compels us to share the Good News of the Gospel.

Sharing the Good News of Jesus Christ is critical and there's no more critical place that this message is needed than India. It's important to understand that India is a land of incredible contrasts. India is home to lavish wealth and extreme poverty. It's a land of extremely intelligent people, and yet millions are illiterate. India is known for Mother Teresa, serving the least and the last. But it's also home to a caste system that perpetuates one of the most abusive social structures on earth, resulting in widespread sex trafficking, child labor, starvation wages, epidemics of rape, and suicides. India's dominant religion (Hinduism) has a reputation for tolerance. But inter-religious conflicts have resulted in millions of violent deaths, and the persecution of Christians continues to intensify. According to research conducted by the Pew Research Center in 2017, of the 198 countries surveyed, India was ranked as the fourth most religiously intolerant nation on earth.

Some powerful political leaders in India would prefer to see Christians eliminated from the country, and some of them even have a timetable to accomplish that. Churches are burned, pastors are murdered, church members are beaten, the homes of Christians are destroyed, and families are intimidated. Some people who become Christians are denied access to wells by the leaders of their villages. Others have been banished from their village, and even from their own families. In extreme cases, family members have tried to kill those who have begun following Jesus.

Despite all of this bad news, believers in India declare that God is sovereign because they have experienced His power, authority, goodness, and constant grace in their lives. They have experienced India's contrasts in ways that most people can hardly imagine. As they now know that God is sovereign, they trust that God's purposes will prevail as they see the Holy Spirit moving through miracles of deliverance.

A 2016 *Christianity Today* cover story declared that India hosts "the world's most vibrant Christward movement." You can visit Calvary Christian Temple in Hyderabad, India and see 25,000 people who fill the auditorium six times every weekend. But as the *Christianity Today* article points out — far more important than a few mega churches — you can also visit any of the tens of thousands of congregations like the one described in the opening line of that article: a group of believers being "led by a barefoot, illiterate father of five."[3]

What does this have to do with the sovereignty of God? What does this have to do with living beyond ourselves? If God is sovereign, do we just let Him take care of things in India while we do our own thing, living in our own insulated world that we have made? Can't we just sit back and let God do His work? What does a sovereign God need us for?

The answer to these questions came to me during a recent trip to Iowa. I was coordinating my flights with a colleague named Josh. Together, we were hosting an event to encourage some of our ministry partners, update them on the ministry, and celebrate all that God was doing in India. Josh and I had booked separate flights on separate airlines, leaving the same day.

Josh arrived on time with no problems. However, things did not turn out so well for me. I missed my first connection because my plane was delayed flying into O'Hare. As I got off the plane in O'Hare, the gate agent told me that if I ran fast, I might catch the next flight and make my next connection. So, I started to run through the airport. There are a lot of things you might want to do to get your exercise, but I can guarantee that running through an airport is not one of them. I ran as fast as I could, but it wasn't fast enough. Weather became a factor, and the delays started piling up. I spent the next twenty-four hours in O'Hare and then they put me on a flight back home. Have you ever slept in an airport? I wouldn't recommend it.

Was God sovereign? Yes! Josh made it to Iowa, and he was just fine. But what about me? God was sovereign over me as well. But make no mistake: The airline was *responsible* for the fact that I never made it to Iowa that day.

As we think about God's love for India, we need to understand that God is *sovereign* over all of human history. But we are still *responsible* within human history. We are responsible for those people who are still walking in darkness, responsible for those living in the land of deep darkness, responsible for those who need to come into the light. That's why we need to live beyond ourselves, and that's why we are empowered to live beyond ourselves. For God is sovereign and all authority is given to Him.

In doing so, we must realize that Isaiah is telling us that there are different levels of darkness. He talks about "walking in darkness" and "living in a land of deep darkness." They are two completely different realities. Before I became a follower of Jesus Christ, I walked in darkness. Even as followers of Christ, my wife and I have walked in dark times. We have walked through the deaths of parents; we have walked through the divorce of close relatives; we have walked through our son Nolan's diagnosis of a brain tumor, and then through the twenty-one years (and counting) of chemo and radiation that followed. As a pastor, I have walked with people through the dark times, whether dealing with prodigal children, a marriage crisis, deaths, or addictions.

Living in a land of deep darkness is an entirely different reality. For many, no rays of light, however tiny, ever penetrate the dark cloud in which they live. There is no light at the end of their tunnel.

This is what I see when I look at India. This is what brought me to Mission India. In fact, this is why Mission India exists!

Mission India trains thousands of India's believers to live beyond themselves by reaching out to those blinded by Satan. Adult Literacy Classes teach roughly 100,000 people every year to read and write. Adult Literacy students learn to grow kitchen gardens and medicinal herbs. They receive lessons in health, social awareness, and income generation through sessions conducted in partnership with local doctors, community health practitioners, and social workers. Children's Bible Clubs reach more than five million children every year with Bible stories, Gospel songs, organized games, and after-school tutoring. On-the-job training of Church Planters reaches unreached villages by presenting the Gospel, establishing prayer groups, and starting thousands of new congregations filled with new believers. In a typical year, more than two million Indians begin to follow Jesus for the first time because of God's work through Mission India.

Jesus is demonstrating His sovereignty in India through these countless miracles. Yet there are still millions who are unreached, who are still living in the land of darkness.

Think about the darkest time in your life. Could you have walked through that valley of darkness without the knowledge of Christ? Without the community of faith or the prayers of believers? Without the Word of God to provide you with comfort and hope? That is unimaginable for many of us. But it is the reality for many people.

Our sovereign God has already done something about this terrible situation. He just told you and me about it. He has told us, "...for to us a child is born, to us a son is given, and the government will be on his shoulders. And his name will be called Wonderful Counselor, Mighty God, Everlasting Father, Prince of Peace" (Isaiah 9:6). We know this, and we know that the rest of the world needs to hear this. So, we must ask, will we live beyond ourselves?

The great message of the Incarnation is that there is no place that Jesus won't go, no depths to which He will not descend, and no darkness that is too dark for His love that transforms all the dark places of our lives.

This is good news because we still live in messy and dark times. But we do not have to be afraid of darkness because Jesus is not afraid of darkness. We can no longer ignore darkness because

Jesus Himself is eager to confront the darkness. Therefore, we live beyond ourselves even when the "beyond" is a dark place. The transforming power of our sovereign God can light up all the darkest places on our planet as His grace empowers us to live beyond ourselves.

If you want to live beyond yourself, you need to trust God fully and abandon anxiety and fear.

Questions for discussion:

1. Read again Isaiah 9:2-7 and Matthew 28:18-20. What do these passages tell us about the sovereignty of God?

2. Why do you think we still struggle with fear and anxiety in our lives? How can we address this challenge in our daily prayers?

3. It's been said that fear is the opposite of faith. Do you agree or disagree? Explain.

4. Think about the darkest time in your life. Could you have walked through that valley of darkness without the knowledge of Christ, without the community of faith or the prayers of believers, without the Word of God to provide you with comfort and hope? What does this suggest about people in India who have none of these resources?

CHAPTER 4:
An Outward Focus

Many thoughtful servants of God have endorsed Henry Blackaby's advice to any follower of Jesus who wants to "experience God": Find out where God is working and go there. Seeking to know the will of God is a human being's most important task. Perhaps the most powerful evidence of what God's will might be — in addition to the testimony of the Scriptures — is to discover where God is working and to join Him there.

I know of no place in the world where this is seen more clearly than in India. God is at work in India in so many different ways, most of them miraculous, and many of them in ways that defy human comprehension. When Mission India first started work in India in the late 1970s, response to evangelistic outreach was dismal. Opposition to the Gospel seemed universal. The physical circumstances of most Christian workers typically included severe poverty and social ostracism.

I'm sure our founder, John DeVries, often questioned how this could be where God was working. Despite all of these negative factors, God was wondrously stirring up the hearts of Indian

Christians. Back then, they were giving testimonies like these:

"I am so happy that I can go every week to three different villages where there is not a single Christian."

"Last month, I was beaten up and told to stay away or face death. Praise the Lord!"

"The first people I led to Christ were excommunicated from their village. They lost their jobs and their homes. But God is good, the church is growing, and we trust Him to provide."

The first work of God has been to raise up passionate workers who understand who God is, have witnessed His power and authority, and are living beyond themselves for the sake of those living in darkness. Nothing deters them. Today, whenever Indian leaders quote Jesus' words, "Pray the Lord to send forth workers into his harvest field," they are quick to add, "God has already answered this prayer. He has raised up thousands of willing workers. They are so eager to reach their countrymen. But often they don't know what to do to reach them. They are desperate for training and the resources."

During the 1980s, hundreds of students enrolled in Mission India's Church Planter Training program. The director of the program said that for every student admitted, there were a dozen more still waiting for training. That ratio has not changed much since then. Despite training more than forty thousand Church Planters since the ministry's inception, Mission India has thousands more on the waiting list. Many of them wait for years for their first chance to be trained to live effectively and strategically beyond themselves.

Mission India staffers have attended hundreds of worship services all over India. We've heard sermons preached by pastors in many different denominations: Pentecostal, Baptist, mainline, and indigenous churches of every imaginable variety. We have yet to hear a sermon calling on God's people to get more active in spreading the Gospel. In most churches in India, such sermons are not necessary. There are already more people living beyond themselves — and more people wanting to become active — than the church's mobilization structures can handle. The harvest fields are surrounded by workers. But, all too often, they are workers without tools and without the knowledge of how to go about bringing in the great harvest that God has prepared.

Of all the stories I've encountered that demonstrate this truth, the story of Saul is my favorite. Not the Saul of the book of Acts, but the Saul of Bhopal, India.

Saul lives in what one might call the "Hindu heartland," where Hinduism and its worldview dominate every community. His hometown, the city of Bhopal, has laws against conversion from Hinduism. Saul was a faithful church member in this hostile environment and he took his faith seriously.

One day, he told his pastor that he felt called by God to bring the Gospel to the rural villages around Bhopal. So, Saul enrolled in Mission India's Church Planter Training.

Saul's training as a Church Planter had established the initial goals for him and taught him the skills to reach them: Walk through the village, witness to six hundred families, and start five prayer groups. Saul prayed. He walked. He witnessed. In response, the villagers spat on him, threw stones at him, and scoffed at his testimony. Not one single person responded by placing faith in Christ. Day after day, Saul met hostility. Week after week, he grew more and more discouraged.

After six months of seemingly fruitless effort, Saul called his wife and confessed his discouragement. He said to her, "Please come and join me. I'm all alone. I need your encouragement. Otherwise, I will just give up this work." Saul's wife and children came to live with him in the village. His wife walked with him, tried to befriend the villagers, and prayed every day for the Lord's blessing.

Still nothing. No positive response. For three more months, they prayed, worked together, and witnessed together. One day, while Saul was out witnessing, some people came to their house and told his wife, "You must leave this place. If you don't leave, someone might kill you." From that day on, people started throwing stones at the house.

Saul decided that this might be the Lord's answer to their prayers for a way to get out. It was time to give up on this village and go elsewhere. As Saul and his wife began packing up their belongings, Saul's shoe broke. So, he walked barefoot to the shoe repairman. While the village cobbler was working on Saul's shoe, the man started sharing with Saul that his daughter was sick and dying. He had taken her to the temple, to the Hindu priest, and they had performed the ceremonies as ordered, but nothing had worked. The cobbler said, "It's just our *karma*. The sins of past lives must have brought this upon us. There is nothing we can do."

Saul said, "May I pray for your daughter? I will ask my God for healing." The cobbler took Saul to his house. When Saul entered the room where this man's daughter lay dying, he saw that she was covered, head to toe, with horrible sores. He put his hands on her and prayed to Jesus. Instantly, the girl began to revive. Within minutes, her sores began to disappear. Saul said, "I prayed to Jesus. I proclaimed the love of Christ, and Jesus demonstrated His love."

What could the cobbler and his wife think? What could they do but acknowledge the loving power of this God? He and his wife, their children, their brothers and sisters, grandparents, aunts, and uncles all began to listen carefully to Saul's testimony. They began to pray to this God of whom they were just learning for the first time. Within a short time, the cobbler's coworkers and neighbors were curious about the miracle, and about the changes they were observing in the cobbler's family.

By the time Saul was celebrating one year of ministry in that village, he had a church of ninety new believers. It has been ten years since that first excursion into a church-planting ministry, and today, Saul and his wife celebrate nine new churches that they have started together. Saul says, "The Lord has given us a vision that before we die, we will start new churches in two hundred villages."

For nine months, there was no life. Yet, today, there is a cascade of people coming alive through the love of Christ. For Indian believers, living beyond themselves is not easy. God does not promise that we will never suffer difficulties, dead ends, and delayed answers to prayer. In the meantime, God might quietly be doing His best work.

My urgent prayer for India is that God will raise up many people who will give and pray beyond themselves, joining themselves to all of the Sauls who are still waiting for the training and equipping they need to reach their fellow citizens with the Good News of Christ.

This is a desperate prayer because much of the North American Church has become so wrapped up in itself that it is no longer aware of God's call to "Go and make disciples of all nations, baptizing them in the name of the Father and of the Son and of the Holy Spirit…" (Matthew 28:19).

We could call this mission drift. It's been happening slowly over the years. The first and second Great Awakening (religious revivals in Britain and the U.S.) led to a wide-scale priority on the Great Commission. The mid-twentieth century, evangelical movement also championed the Great Commission as it gave birth to numerous parachurch ministries and relief organizations which focused on reaching unreached people groups.

But something has changed over time. If you understand the Great Commission and pray for its advancement, advocate with others to engage in it, and generously give to its expansion, you represent a small percentage of Christians.

Are you familiar with the name George Barna? He founded Barna Group, one of the premier research organizations in the United States. They did a study in 2018 and even wrote a book on their findings all centered around the Great Commission.[4] They wanted to know what percentage of regular, North American church members understood and were engaged in the Great Commission. Barna Group asked regular church attendees if they could articulate the Great Commission. Of those surveyed, 51 percent said no, 25 percent had heard of it but weren't sure what it meant, 17 percent said yes and were able to define it, and 6 percent weren't sure what it meant. Barna then considered that, perhaps, the phrase "Great Commission" was not being used or talked about as it had been in the past. So they presented the church attendees with five verses from Scripture and asked them to identify which one was about the

Great Commission. The results improved, but not by much: 37 percent correctly identified the text; the rest simply did not know or gave a wrong answer.

We still have Christ's call. We still sing hymns and worship songs, highlighting the call of the Great Commission and the call of the life of Christ. But despite these truths, we're drifting away from the call. David Bosch, in his book *Transforming Mission: Paradigm Shifts in Theology of Mission*, says, "There is a church because there is a mission, not vice-versa."[5] Barna Group goes on to suggest that this is not just about knowing the Great Commission so we can get an A on a survey; this is about being who Christ calls us to be and doing the work of the Gospel that the Holy Spirit empowers us to do. For this to happen, we need advocates and ambassadors.

We all need to be Kingdom connectors, encouraging people to be actively involved in advancing the Kingdom of God. According to Barna Group's findings, the need is more urgent today than at any other time. So, I ask you right now to talk to your friends and pastors. Start to pray right now and ask God to give you names of people whom you need to speak with about engaging in the Great Commission. Pray that God would give you an open door to advocate for the Great Commission. Start first by encouraging and celebrating those who are engaging in it and offer to help, pray, and walk with them. I hope you agree that we can't just sit idly by while 2.8 billion people remain unreached by the Gospel throughout the world.

When you begin to live beyond yourself, your focus becomes outward. You seek to reach those who are still outside of God's Kingdom.

Questions for discussion:

1. What do you find most inspiring about the story of Saul of Bhopal?

2. Have you seen evidence of "mission drift" in your church community or in your own life? Why, or why not?

3. List different ways that you can pray for the Kingdom of God.

CHAPTER 5:
God's Kingdom; Our Kingdom

In the first eleven chapters of the Bible, we see Satan doing his best to ruin God's good creation and His call to humanity to co-rule and co-reign with Him in establishing His Kingdom (Genesis 1:27-30). The desire we each have to build our own kingdoms is one of Satan's strategies to ruin whatever is good in God's creation. In the stories of Scripture, we see this desire unfold in sibling rivalry, prison, famine, murders, deceit, floods, sexual immorality, and abuse of power, which are all part of our attempts to build human kingdoms in the place of God's sovereign rule.

This reaches its culmination in the Exodus story. In this story, people have forgotten who God is and what He promises. They have forgotten the miracles of Joseph's story. Powerful Egyptian rulers mistreat the Hebrew people, and the book of Exodus unveils their horrible situation. The name of God is not even mentioned in the first seventeen verses of the book, suggesting the complete godlessness of that time and place, and the complete disregard for the blessing that God gave in Genesis 1:28.

Whenever I read these seventeen verses, I think of India. It's as if India has been living Exodus chapter one for thousands of years. The people of India lift up and worship 330 million gods. The fear and hopelessness generated by these gods have led to unimaginable suffering, poverty, mistreatment of the poor, abuse of women, corruption at all levels of society, and the fragmentation of families, communities, and ethnic groups.

Among the world's more than 9,000 people groups, more than 4,000 are unreached by the Gospel. According to the 2011 Census of India, India tops the list of most unreached people groups with 1,900 such groups — that is, four times as many as China, the second most unreached nation.

Some people, when they hear these facts, think, "What a hopeless situation!" Others think, "What an incredible opportunity!" There is an aspect of India's extreme need that supports the perspective of the optimists.

Around 2010, Mission India came across an intriguing map produced by the International Mission Board of the Southern Baptist Convention. "The Global Status of Evangelical Christianity," as the map is called, plotted out population centers and people groups on a world map and color coded them based on how much (or how little) Gospel penetration had taken place in each area. Places where at least 10 percent of the local population were followers of Christ were green, and as that percentage dropped, the color turned from green to yellow, and yellow to orange, and finally, orange to red. The darker the color, the more unreached that people group or population center was. The result was a fascinating picture of the most unreached and unengaged places on our planet. The nation of India stuck out like a sore thumb. It was saturated in red. Turn to the back of this book to see what I mean.

We've been referring to that map ever since. While it continues to motivate us to reach the nation of India for Christ, it also serves as a great encouragement — because the map is changing. We've watched the data change many of those red dots in India from red to orange to yellow and even green. And while a green dot (representing 10 percent evangelized) hardly means the work is done, it reflects the incredible growth and spiritual openness in India of which we've been witnesses! And *that* is something to celebrate.

If I were in the gold mining business, I would go where the gold is. If I were in the diamond business, I would go where the diamonds are. But God has called us into the soul-winning business, the business of reaching the unreached. So, He is calling us to establish His Kingdom where the unreached souls are located, where the most people in the most places know the least about the Good News of the Kingdom.

In the book of Exodus, God was in the business of delivering Israel from oppression. So, He went where the need was, and He began to do His work.

"Now Joseph and all his brothers and all that generation died, but the Israelites were exceedingly fruitful; they multiplied greatly, increased in numbers and became so numerous that the land was filled with them" (Exodus 1:6-7). The growth of Israel showed that the Lord was at work, building up the families of His chosen people. And then, in Exodus 2, God hears the intercessory prayers and cries of His people, and He starts working out His plan of deliverance. We can't miss this principle: Wherever people pray, God works.

What we must understand is that prayer is always the first work of missions. Where people pray, God works. Notice that God answered the prayers of every young Israelite wife, of every young husband. Notice the words "fruitful" and "multiplied." God is a multiplying, fruit-giving God who is building His holy nation, making them so numerous that the Egyptians begin to fear their power.

Whenever God's people align their lives with Him, God is always at work, bringing forth the reality of His rule. The map of India, located at the back of this book, was produced in 2010. Since then, God's people have been praying and working to bring the Good News to India's lost. The Holy Spirit has been at work with them. Between 2002 and 2018, Mission India's 1,500 partners saw over 26.6 million Indians profess faith in Christ. Since Mission India's inception, over 170,000 churches have been established. Along with many other Christian workers in India, we have been used by God to change the spiritual landscape of India.

As India's new believers are living beyond themselves — sometimes in the face of fierce opposition — God's agenda is advancing to transform India from a land of darkness to a land of light. We are not there yet, but the evidence is overwhelming. God has His sights set on India, and He is using all kinds of people. And, often, He chooses the people we would least expect.

It was on my first trip to India as president of Mission India that I met Raju Joseph, a Church Planter whom God is using in a powerful way. Raju was a rag picker, scouring the landfill near his small hut for anything he could sell to a recycler. He earned just $1 per day. Life was hard for Raju, and it had been that way for as long as he could remember.

When Raju was just a young boy, his father was dying while Raju was at school. By the time Raju came home, his father was already gone. Filled with anger, Raju ran to a railway station and found an empty car, climbed inside, and fell asleep. When he woke up, he was hundreds of miles away from everything he knew.

Lost and alone, he quickly fell into the grip of poverty and injustice. He traveled around and worked several jobs but was never paid fairly for his work. He was beaten and abused. He spent time in jail. A desire arose in his heart to raise his voice against these injustices, to fight and stop them. Raju protested and argued, but nothing changed. People responded by mistreating him and forcing him to move. Raju didn't realize this at the time, but God was preparing to use his brokenness to give him a voice to proclaim God's mercy and justice.

During this time, Raju met a pastor named Anup, who shared the Word of God with him. Raju's heart was transformed, specifically by Romans 10. Raju was baptized, and now he lives to share God's grace with others.

As a new Christian, Raju took on a new name: Joseph. Emerging from a pit in Raju Joseph's own life, God was preparing to use him in a mighty way. Motivated by the love of Jesus, Raju Joseph began working tirelessly for his community. As a result of his efforts, a well was installed in his village. Neighbors received food-ration cards. Electricity was added to the village, and neighbors finally had rights to their land. An entire community began experiencing the transformational love of Jesus for the first time. Today, the power of God is present in this area as He works through one simple man, living boldly for Christ.

Raju Joseph trusts God to touch every aspect of life and community. God has big goals, and Raju Joseph wants to be part of seeing those come to pass. When you align yourself with God's big goals, you are living beyond yourself in the best way possible. God will honor that and do great things through you.

How great? Well, how great are God's goals?

In Isaiah 49, a conversation between Isaiah and God takes place during a low point in Israel's history and a low point in the prophet's life. Isaiah says, "'I have labored in vain; I have spent my strength for nothing at all. Yet what is due me is in the Lord's hand, and my reward is with my God'" (Isaiah 49:4).

God's response to Isaiah in Isaiah 49:6 is classic. He does not say, "That's ok, Isaiah. I know you're discouraged. Here's a little pat on the back." Instead, God tells Isaiah that the real problem is in his own mind. He wasn't thinking big enough. "It is too small a thing for you to be my servant to restore the tribes of Jacob and bring back those of Israel I have kept. I will also make you a light for the Gentiles, that my salvation may reach to the ends of the earth."

Every time I read this text, I hear God saying, "You're not thinking big enough! It is not a big enough job for my servant just to recover the lost tribes of Jacob and merely round up the strays of Israel. I am setting you up as a light for all the nations so that my salvation becomes global."

When we start living beyond ourselves, we abandon our small goals and limited perspective. We start thinking big. We start to see the world as God sees it, and to trust that we can contribute to God's big goals to bring His Kingdom into every realm of life and every place on the planet.

It's more than a magic ticket for eternal life. A good example comes from the movie *Monty Python and the Holy Grail*, a movie about King Arthur and his knight, Sir Lancelot, who are seeking after the holy grail. As they go about this quest, they come to a bridge that spans an abyss of eternal peril. A bridge keeper allows people to cross this bridge only if they can answer three questions correctly. Get one wrong and you are tossed into the pit. Sir Lancelot is first to test the bridge keeper. The keeper asks him what his name is. Sir Lancelot answers. When asked what his quest is, Sir Lancelot responds by talking about his journey to seek the holy grail. When asked what his favorite color is, Sir Lancelot answers "blue" and immediately the bridge keeper lets him cross. Sir Lancelot crosses the bridge amazed, thinking how easy it was.

Similarly, the second knight states his name and quest. But the third question changes to "What is the capital of Assyria?" Suddenly, the knight, not knowing the answer, is hurled, screaming into the abyss. The third knight is nervous as he is asked his name and quest. But he answers correctly. When it comes time to answer what his favorite color is, he panics, "Blue, no yellow, no — ahh!" Immediately, He falls into the pit.

Finally, King Arthur steps up. By the time he gets to the third question, it's been changed to "What is the air speed velocity of an unladen swallow?" King Arthur responds with, "What do you mean? An African swallow or a European swallow?" The bridge keeper doesn't know the answer, so, immediately, he is launched into the abyss. King Arthur and his followers thereafter cross the bridge unhindered.

Many people's idea of the Kingdom of God is just like that: Someday, we will get to a bridge to paradise and be asked why we should be allowed to cross. Somewhere along the way, we redefined the "Kingdom of God" into some sort of minimum entrance requirement for getting into Heaven.

Rather than expecting the Kingdom of God to revolutionize lives, we put it off, thinking personal salvation today and the Kingdom of God will happen in Heaven tomorrow. In the midst of that, we miss God and a sense of destiny for our lives and the calling of the Church.

What God said to Isaiah, He is also saying to us: "I will also make you a light for the Gentiles, that my salvation may reach to the ends of the earth" (Isaiah 49:6).

If you want to live beyond yourself, your life should be aligned with God's agenda, God's big goal. That's when miracles happen. We have to become ambassadors of the Great Commission.

Questions for discussion:

1. Read again Isaiah 49:1-6. Have you ever felt like Isaiah, thinking you "have labored in vain" and "spent [your] strength for nothing at all"? What does God's answer to

Isaiah in verse 6 suggest about the point of our labors?

2. Look again at the map of India mentioned in this chapter. What strikes you most about this map? Is there anything in this map that surprises you?

3. In your own words, what is "God's big goal"?

4. What does the story of Raju Joseph suggest to you about living beyond yourself? How does this relate to "God's big goal"?

CHAPTER 6:
Prayer: The First Work of Living Beyond Yourself

When I was fifteen years old, my attitude was all out of whack, like many teens my age. I was a challenge for my parents. Perhaps I was not so unusual. Perhaps you can relate! If you can't remember what you were like back then, ask your parents, or think back to your own fifteen-year-old child.

I remember walking into the living room one evening and finding my mom on her knees at the couch. The tears were running down her face. I heard her say my name *out loud*. She didn't know that I had walked into the room. She was praying for me.

As you can imagine, that experience made a huge impact on me as a teenager. But even more impactful than hearing my mom's prayers for me were the ways that God has answered those prayers over the years. God answered in ways that neither she nor I could have predicted.

Since then, there have been hundreds of times when I've realized how much I needed others to pray for me, and, thankfully, people have been there at those important points in my life. By God's grace, I've been surrounded by people who know Jesus and who believe in Jesus' promise to answer prayers that they offer on my behalf.

My experience of being prayed into the Kingdom by my mother is often reversed in India. There, many parents are prayed into the Kingdom by their children!

I was standing in a crowded slum once during a trip to India, talking to a little boy and his parents. Suraj, only eleven years old, is one of six family members living in a rented room less than ten feet wide. They do not have running water or a bathroom. Their room has a single light bulb and a dirt floor. They used to live in their own house in a rural village, but now they live in a big city slum.

Suraj told me, "My father, Ganesh, used to drink a lot. When he was drunk, he beat my mother without mercy. He was also a gambler and had many debts. We lost our house and our land to his gambling."

Suraj's mother, Manju, explained, "There was always so much shouting in our house. I cried a lot."

"When my father beat my mother, sometimes, she would run away in desperation," Suraj shared. "Then, I would go out and bring her back. Sometimes, my father also beat me when I came between them to stop him from hitting my mother."

The end result of this chaos? Manju said, "We lost everything in our life, including our house and our property. We were miserable."

Suraj's mother insisted that he attend school, but Suraj refused to learn. He often skipped his classes. Manju sensed her son's broken spirit and was desperate. When she learned about the Year-Long Children's Bible Club in the neighborhood that included free tutoring, she signed him up.

Suraj said, "I came to the club with tears on my face. My teacher, Seeta, asked me why I was so sad. I told her about my drunkard father and the trouble he was causing us, how we tried our best but could not get him to quit his bad habits."

In the Bible Club, Suraj learned stories of Jesus. Seeta taught him how to pray to Jesus. Suraj started asking the Lord every day to intervene in Ganesh's life. Suraj said, "I prayed, 'Please God, change my father.' Every day, I prayed this prayer."

One day, a miracle happened. For the first time, Ganesh came home sober. It did not happen immediately, but, within a few months, he had stopped drinking completely, stopped gambling, and found a job as a rickshaw driver. Suraj says, "God heard my prayers and, now, my father is a totally new man. Now, he works every day and brings his earnings home."

Ganesh and Suraj both decided to start following Jesus. Today, their entire family is praying to Jesus daily in their home. Ganesh says, "My drinking caused many problems in our home. Suraj prayed for me. He asked God to fill our home with peace and to lead us on the right path. Then, I prayed to God and started reading the Bible. When I read the Bible, I was overwhelmed. I felt that there was hope again. I am so proud of my son. If Suraj had never joined the Bible Club, my children would still be distressed and starving. And I would still be a drunkard."

Stories like this are being written all over India. God is answering thousands of child-like prayers and bringing thousands of parents into the Kingdom of God. Of course, as followers of Jesus, we all know that we need to pray for others. But we get busy. We get distracted. We have good intentions, and, now and then, we try to do it. We want to do it more often. We want to get better at it, to be more faithful. For most of us, it's not so easy.

There are some believers who pray frequently, consistently, and for long periods of time. It's just like breathing for them. For others, it's as natural as singing. But, for most of us, it's harder than it should be.

I no longer remember my mom's exact words as she prayed for me on her knees. But knowing my mom, I know this: Her prayers were offered over and over. The main thing she prayed for was my relationship with Jesus. She prayed beyond herself. She prayed that Jesus would become the Lord of my life. And the Lord answered those prayers.

Do we really believe in the power of prayer?

There are many great examples in Scripture that encourage us to believe; my favorite is found in Acts 12. Peter had just been thrown into prison by King Herod, who seemed to be firmly in control. He had all the political clout. He was commander in chief. He set the trials, ordered executions, and determined the fate of anyone he chose.

Get the details of the scene in your mind. Herod has assigned four squads of armed soldiers to guard Peter. He has a guard chained to his left hand. He has a guard chained to his right hand. There are two more guards right outside the cell, and at least two more guards outside the door of the prison itself. At night, they shut the iron gates to lock everyone inside.

Luke painstakingly lays out for us the hopelessness of Peter's situation. Perhaps this reminds some of us of the hopelessness of our own situation, the hopelessness of our marriage, or our finances, or maybe an addiction, or a medical condition. Yet Luke wants us to know that there is hope in the face of hopelessness. Sometimes, hopelessness is God's gift to us, to motivate us to connect to His power. While Peter sat in that heavily-guarded cell, his brothers and sisters in Christ were earnestly praying for him.

This is all about God's power at work, what God can do when His people pray. Sometimes, we get into this mindset of "If I just do it right...." And we think, "If it's to be, it's up to me." But that's not the way prayer works at all. When our prayers bless others, it's because of the power of God at work. So, when you pray, you can relax.

Peter is so at peace that he's sound asleep. When the angel comes, he has to hit Peter to wake him up. Even after the chains have fallen off and Peter has gotten dressed, followed the angel past the guards, and walked through the iron gate, which has opened by itself, Peter is still so passive and groggy, he thinks he is dreaming.

Peter's experience demonstrates the fulfillment of Solomon's prayer in 1 Chronicles 29:11: "Yours, Lord, is the greatness and the power and the glory and the majesty and the splendor, for everything in heaven and earth is yours. Yours, Lord, is the kingdom; you are exalted as head over all." Prayers that bless others originate in our understanding of God's absolute power.

Not every Christian understands this. Theologian Hans Kung wrote a book titled *On Being a Christian*. Kung left out one key ingredient in this book: prayer. When Kung was asked why, he said, "I forgot."[6] Some of us get so caught up in our own agendas that we forget about the greatest power in the universe. We forget to live and pray beyond ourselves.

How do you know when you're depending on your own power? For me, it's obvious. I get emotionally, spiritually, and even physically worn out. Fatigue can be a warning sign that you are depending on your own power to fix things, rather than depending on God.

We can't forget that we have access to the Creator of the universe: The one who parted the Red Sea, who raised the dead and made the blind to see! We can only understand His power if we understand Him. This understanding only comes from spending time with Him, reading His Word, and searching to know His will.

Peter's powerful prayer experience started before he was arrested. His incarceration was not an accident of history. God's decision to free him was not only because of God's love for Peter. God's decision arose out of God's love for those unnamed people whom Peter was reaching with the Good News of the Kingdom. God had given Peter a mandate, and those who imprisoned Peter were trying to block that agenda.

God answered Suraj's prayers — the drunkard's son — because God wanted Suraj's parents in the Kingdom. God answered the prayers for Peter because so many people were waiting to hear the Good News that Peter wanted to share with them.

This is why the Apostle Paul so often asks people to pray for him, "...that I will fearlessly make known the mystery of the Gospel..." (Ephesians 6:19). Those prayers were not for Paul's benefit. Those were prayers for people who didn't yet know the truth about God, those who needed to hear Paul's Good News and start following Jesus. Paul was living beyond himself, and he was asking people to pray beyond themselves.

Thinking about unbelievers can be discouraging. No one can force another person to receive Jesus. Satan has a powerful grip on the secular agnostics that surround us in America. He seems to have a powerful grip on the Muslims and Hindus around the world who have never encountered the power of God in their lives, never heard the truth, and never had the opportunity to make a decision to follow Jesus. It seems as hopeless for them as it was for Peter in that dark prison.

At Mission India, we do our best to design programs to reach the unreached. But, unless the Holy Spirit goes before us, there will be no rejoicing in Heaven over those who come to faith.

Suraj reminds us that it's never hopeless, that the Holy Spirit is ready to do incredible miracles as He answers our prayers.

The drunkard and his son did not receive what God had to give them until the drunkard's son began to ask for it. James 4:2 says, "You do not have because you do not ask God."

In light of this, let's pray a special prayer right now. I invite you to do it this very minute. I am confident that, in this moment, multitudes of Indian Christians are praying, and I want to invite you to join with them.

This prayer is based on Matthew 8:1-4, where a leper says to Jesus, "If you are willing, you can make me clean." Jesus responds by saying, "I am willing" and he touched the leper. The leper was blessed in five ways: His body, his labor, his emotions, his social life, and his spiritual life were all blessed. This story illustrates what Jesus can do for an individual or even for a neighborhood.

All over India, new believers take their first steps as baby Christians with this new habit: Holding up the five fingers of their right hand, they list five people that they are praying for; holding up the five fingers of their left hand, they list the prayers that they pray every day, using the acronym B.L.E.S.S. to guide them.

The B.L.E.S.S. Prayer

Jesus, please bless my family and these five neighbors:

B: Bless their *Bodies* with health;

L: Bless their *Labor* and work;

E: Bless their *Emotions* with peace and joy;

S: Bless them *Socially* with love for others;

S: Bless them *Spiritually* with salvation and Heaven;

For your sake, Jesus. Amen.

It's no accident that the Good News is spreading fast through the villages and communities of India. I imagine miracles of answered prayers multiplying exponentially as each new believer prays prayers that ultimately leads more people into the Kingdom of God.

Early on in Mission India's history, our founder, John DeVries, was asked by a very wealthy man, "John, what is the greatest need of the ministry?" John paused and finally answered, "Prayer is our greatest need; I simply need more intercessors." I stand with John on this belief because prayer can do what only God can do. And we pray big prayers.

I read an article recently that really reinforced this for me. The point that the author made was that anyone who has been engaged in cross-cultural missions begins to experience a shift in focus in the ministry. It starts to become more and more about prayer. I know this is true in my life. I have a prayer group I pray with every Sunday evening. I also have a prayer team of around 150 people who pray for me and Mission India twice per month. What's more, the staff of Mission and our partners in India gather for prayer every day.

We trust in the powerful words of Ephesians 3:20, which are: "Now to him who is able to do immeasurably more than all we ask or imagine, according to his power that is at work within us." God's immeasurable love for Mission India was, yet again, evidenced by an encounter I experienced.

Early on in 2018, a friend of mine encouraged me to contact a man I'll call Pete. He was a person of influence and affluence connected to my friend's organization. He told me that Pete was a man of high capacity and, more importantly, had a heart for the Great Commission in India. Sounds great, right? But here's where things got tricky. My friend was unable to introduce me to Pete. It had to happen organically. Without any common denominator, I began to strategize how I would get in front of Pete.

I contacted friends whom I thought might run in the same circles as Pete and asked if anyone might know him and be willing to make an introduction. Unfortunately, my contacts came up empty. I remember saying to one of them, "Well, all we have left is prayer."

Fast forward six weeks to the Issachar Summit, a conference where Kingdom leaders meet with business and professional leaders for exposure to the latest thinking in world missions and evangelism. I had been asked to serve as a table leader at the summit and was required to attend a training event before the conference began. To be honest, I did not want to serve as a table leader because it meant one more night away from home. But I went because I thought it would be a great opportunity. At the training event, there were fourteen tables and I ended up sitting next to a gentleman from Detroit. We chatted about family, the Great Commission, and the summit. Nearly one hour went by and I still hadn't caught his name. Toward the end of our conversation, I noticed his nametag, "Pete." This was proof that God was working through prayers.

Once we made the connection that I worked for Mission India, Pete mentioned that he had researched our ministry. It turned out that Pete had recently traveled to India and sensed its need for the Gospel. Pete had also felt the urge to research the ministries that are spreading the Good News of Jesus Christ in this unreached nation. At the end of our conversation, he handed me his card and encouraged me to call him so we could talk about a potential partnership.

If you want to live beyond yourself, you must first learn the power of prayer. The first thing you do when you start to live beyond yourself is to pray. Prayer is always the first work of missions. Before anything else, pray.

Questions for discussion:

1. What did you like best about this chapter? What, if anything, did you find confusing or hard to understand?

2. Think of a neighbor, coworker, or acquaintance who does not know Christ or who is struggling in his or her faith. Write down how you will pray the B.L.E.S.S. Prayer for that person:

B: Bless their *Bodies* with health;

L: Bless their *Labor* and work;

E: Bless their *Emotions* with peace and joy;

S: Bless them *Socially* with love for others;

S: Bless them *Spiritually* with salvation and Heaven.

3. Could you pray this way for them every day over the next five weeks? (Be prepared to witness God's miraculous answer to your prayers.)

CHAPTER 7:
There is Power in Your Prayers

Now that we've covered the importance of prayer, we need to respond to the question: How do you move forward if you feel frustrated when you experience an unanswered prayer? If you've lost faith in the power of your prayers or if you are wondering how to experience the power of prayer, ask God to teach you.

Earlier, I shared the story of our adopting Jori. Our adoption process started when I was forty-four years old; Jean was forty-two. Once we had decided to adopt, we knew God was calling us to adopt from India. (That seed was planted years ago on my first visit to India.) We eagerly filled out all the paperwork, did the home study, went through the necessary training, asked for reference letters, and were finally accepted. Then, we started praying.

To be specific, I prayed for a girl. I took a photo of a little Indian girl and put it in a prominent place on my desk. I prayed every time I looked at it. For an entire year, Jean and I, along with our kids, faithfully prayed. And what happened? Nothing. Year two: We prayed and started asking our church and friends to pray.

Nothing. Year three: We started to add fasting to our prayers. Still nothing.

One month into the third year of praying, we received an email. The email contained the photographs and the medical files of three little girls. It informed us that we had four hours to make a decision: Which child did we want?

We sensed God leading us to pick baby number two. We were so excited that we showed her picture to everyone. Our family and friends started praying even harder, and our church was praying that the process to bring her home would be quick.

Our family started making plans and dreaming of the future. One week stretched into another. One month into another. We waited … and waited. Eight months later, we finally got the phone call from the case worker who said, "The two of you need to sit down. The Indian government says she is too healthy; you can't have her. But the process does allow you to appeal."

We were devastated. We didn't know what to do. We told our children and our family. Everyone was in a state of disbelief. We decided to appeal and to keep praying. The answer came back again: This girl cannot be adopted by an American family.

With the advice of our caseworker and with the help of the director of the orphanage, we appealed again. And again, we were denied. We were not just distraught, we were heartbroken and disappointed in God. But we kept praying. I have not had this happen often in my life, but as I prayed one day, God told me that Jori would someday be in our home. I knew it was God's voice and I was confident it would all work out.

We had one appeal left. Our caseworker warned us that the government officials were getting tired of hearing from us. So, one Sunday morning, we shared our entire situation with our church and asked them to pray specifically for a miraculous breakthrough. A church member later approached us and said, "My wife and I support a missionary who happens to live near the orphanage. Can we tell him about your problem?"

Within one week, the missionary emailed back to inform us that the Head of State Adoption just happened to attend his Bible study. He asked for our permission to approach him with our problem. I don't know if the Head of State Adoption pulled some strings or made some calls, but I know that, a short time later, our caseworker called and said, "Your appeal has been granted." Four years and one month from the time we started praying, we brought Jori home.

Looking back, that ordeal taught me an important lesson: There is a big difference between "no" and "not yet." There are verses in the Bible that I don't particularly like but have learned to believe: "Consider it pure joy, my brothers and sisters, whenever you face trials of many kinds, because you know that the testing of your faith produces perseverance. Let perseverance finish its work so that you may be mature and complete, not lacking anything" (James 1:2-4).

What I know now is that God intended all along to bring Jori into our family. But we needed to feel powerless so that He would get the glory. He intended all along to overcome the obstacles. But He wanted us to trust Him completely so that when it happened, we would give the credit where the credit was due. He intended all along to build up our faith, to grow our capacity to persevere, and to grow us in our maturity in Christ.

When God answers our prayers, we need to tell others what He has done. This gives God glory and it increases the faith of others. There are so many stories I could share of God answering my prayers. I could go on and on about Jori, India, finances .... But the story I want to share next is about a prayer I prayed for my wife, Jean.

About ten years ago, while pastoring a church in Michigan, a church in California offered me a position. We felt God leading us to accept it; so, we did. We began preparing for the move by selling things we didn't need and saying goodbye to friends and family, including Jean's longtime employer and the church that we had poured our lives into for ten years. Our oldest daughter, Ashley, would be staying in Michigan. So, we shared a gut-wrenching goodbye with her, too.

When we got to California, we were still in "change mode." Our kids were at a new school, we were in a new community, and I had a new job. While I enjoyed my new role and loved the mission of the church, Jean was still feeling quite lonely. Without Ashley and her close friends and family members, she had a hard time finding joy.

Late one night, I was lying awake because I couldn't sleep, thinking about Jean. So, I got up and started to pray. During my prayer, I flashed back to twenty years earlier when Jean and I served for a summer in Philadelphia. We met a woman there named Kirsten, who was from southern California. Kirsten and Jean quickly became friends. In fact, the next year, Kirsten even flew to Michigan to spend Christmas with our family. The two kept in touch for many years, but then came kids, work, and life, and they slowly lost touch.

I became determined to find her for Jean's sake. I tried searching Google and social media but couldn't locate her. I even called the organization for which we had volunteered in Philadelphia to see if they had any contact information for her. Nothing. The only thing I could do was pray.

I pleaded for God to make a way to help us find Kirsten. But more than that, I prayed that God would bless Jean with rich relationships. I prayed that prayer for a long time.

Months later, we were at our kids' school for a parent night. We were going through our son Luke's classes, meeting his teachers, and hearing about what would be taught in the upcoming year. When we walked into Luke's history class, I saw a woman out of the corner of my eye and the thought went through my mind that she looked familiar. As I had met so many people since moving to the area, I was trying to place how I might know her. But nothing clicked. All of a sudden I heard, "Todd VanEk! Is that you?" It was Kirsten! Jean and I couldn't believe our eyes. We were so excited!

Remember Jean had no idea I was searching for Kirsten. Nor did she know I was praying for God's intervention in her life. Just imagine this scene of celebration after twenty years of separation.

I picture God thinking, "Todd, I don't need your help in this. I know where Kirsten is and I know where Jean is. I am the gracious one, the compassionate one, the merciful one, and I will orchestrate Jean's life and I will bring good to her." That's exactly who God is. In that instant, God broke through and showed His graciousness. I think that's what prayer does. Prayer helps us see who God is, and that provides a way for us to share our prayer journey with others.

God intends to train and empower His people in India to bring the Gospel to every corner of the subcontinent. He intends to heal the sick, answer prayers, and perform mighty miracles in the name of Jesus. He wants to free the oppressed, to comfort the widows and orphans, to enlarge His heavenly family with millions of Indians. But *He* wants the glory so others will know who He is and discover His goodness and grace. He wants His people to persevere, to mature in their faith as a witness to others. He is just waiting for His people to pray, to intercede, to ask for the right things, and to keep on asking.

I have listened to hundreds of testimonies from Indians who share the details of how they came to know Christ. Every single one of them has expressed some kind of surprising experience of Jesus' power in his or her life. "I was sick. A brother prayed to Jesus for me, and I was healed"; "I was jobless. Believers prayed for me, and now I'm able to support my family"; "I was suicidal, in such desperate straits that I wanted to end it all. My sister prayed for me, and I've never had such peace, such joy as Jesus has given me and my family."

God wants to do great things in India. He wants to do great things in us. He is just waiting for us to ask Him. When we feel our own need deeply, we are more likely to pray.

Indian believers don't know any different. For so many of them, they have no alternative but to believe the promise of James 5:14: "Is anyone among you sick? Let them call the elders of the church to pray over them and anoint them with oil in the name of the Lord. And the prayer offered in faith will make the sick person well."

This is the Church — gathered together, praying in community, sharing their struggles, agreeing in Jesus' name, and receiving

Jesus' answers.

How are we as the Church doing at praying together? How are you? How am I? How are we at sharing what's going on in our lives, saying, "This is where I need prayer"? I have grown up hearing people giving an answer to the question, "How are you doing?" They almost always say, "fine," even when they aren't fine. Maybe they thought that they were the only ones who were struggling. They're not.

Looking at the prayers in the Bible, it's surprising how often the actual prayers aren't recorded. Acts 12:5 says, "…but the church was earnestly praying to God…" but we're not told what they were saying. Verse 12 says, "…many people had gathered and were praying." Many times the Bible just says, "so and so prayed"; "Jesus went off to a quiet place to pray"; "Moses and Joshua went off to pray"; "The whole assembly prayed"; "They prayed without ceasing."

Don't you wish we had the words? If we did, we might feel like we had the secret code, the words that can get God's attention. *If I can just use these words with this tone of voice, then God will pay attention.*

But there is a promise in the Bible that is one hundred times better than a prayer formula. This promise — more than any other — helps me to let go and let God: "…the moment we get tired in the waiting, God's Spirit is right alongside helping us along. If we don't know how or what to pray, it doesn't matter. He does our praying in and for us, making prayer out of our hopeless sighs, our aching groans" (See Romans 8:26).

Sometimes, the most articulate prayers you can pray are your tears rolling down your face (Acts 20:31). Then, the Holy Spirit takes all the emotions, all the words — expressed and unexpressed — and puts them into words before God.

Several years ago, I read an article about John Wimber, founding pastor of the Vineyard movement. Vineyard churches have long been known for their healing services where people with all kinds of sickness come to be prayed for, asking for miraculous healing. It's not just Wimber or the church leaders who do the praying; everyone in the church prays for healing.

Wimber had shared that he was dying of cancer. When asked if he still believed in healing even though he was dying of cancer, he responded by explaining his desire for miraculous healing in the lives of others. Most of the people he prayed for weren't healed, but many were. He pointed out that in every case prayer helped. God uses prayer to comfort, encourage, and strengthen our faith, or to lift our spirit.

A short time later, Wimber died. Wimber could not, nor can anyone else, detail the impact of the thousands of prayers that were offered on his behalf. And, of course, Wimber is now healed in Heaven!

Rick Warren, one of my favorite leaders, shared that some scientists have looked at the impact that prayers have on the recovery of a patient, even if the patient doesn't know he or she is being prayed for. The most famous study was done by Dr. Randolph Byrd at the University of California. He took nearly four hundred cardiac patients that had come in with heart attacks and put half of them in a study group. He didn't tell anyone he had done this. He took about two hundred names and gave them to people all across the country along with the request: "Pray for these people." The people who were praying didn't know the patients. The patients didn't know that they were being prayed for, neither did the doctors or nurses. They all got the same state-of-the-art, high-level cardiac medical treatment. But half were being prayed for, and half were not. Only the researchers knew it.

Those who were prayed for were less likely to develop congestive heart failure, five times less likely to require antibiotics, three times less likely to need diuretics, and less likely to require a breathing tube. Fewer of those being prayed for developed pneumonia, fewer needed CPR, and none of those who were being prayed for died. A medical researcher stated, "If the therapy being evaluated had been a new drug, it would undoubtedly have been heralded as a medical breakthrough."[7]

You don't have to know the people for whom you are praying, and they don't have to know you. God knows, God cares, and God answers. Indians often write to me with the request, "Who can we pray for? We want to pray for the people who are praying for us." They are totally comfortable praying for strangers.

Perhaps our greatest challenge in India is sustaining our prayers for people we have never met, whose names we don't know, and whose situations we can hardly imagine.

Perhaps our second greatest challenge is believing when God answers.

Acts 12:12-15 tells us that when Peter was miraculously released from prison, "...he went to the house of Mary the mother of John, also called Mark, where many people had gathered and were praying. Peter knocked at the outer entrance, and a servant girl named Rhoda came to answer the door. When she recognized Peter's voice, she was so overjoyed that she ran back without opening it and exclaimed, 'Peter is at the door!' 'You're out of your mind,' they told her. When she kept insisting that it was so, they said, 'It must be his angel.'"

I've told thousands of people the stories of God's miracles in India. Sometimes, I get the impression that many just don't believe them. Surely, it defies belief that our ministry partners planted eleven thousand new churches in a single year, or, during the same year, that they recorded two million new believers, or, that a woman was healed of leprosy, or, a boy healed of cancer, or, thousands of parents came to believe in Jesus because of the testimonies of their own children. There must be some other explanation!

The church in Acts 12 finally opened the door. When Peter walked in, they realized what the Lord had done. Someday, when Heaven's doors are opened, we will all witness with our own eyes and ears what God has done in India and across the globe.

If you want to live beyond yourself, you need to pray for specific needs. God wants to do great things. He wants to do great things through us and through our prayers. He wants to bless others through us. He is just waiting for us to ask Him. Trust in the power of the Holy Spirit, working through your own prayers — and He will work through you.

Questions for discussion:

1. The story of adopting Jori is an example of God giving the answer "not yet" rather than "no." Can you share an experience that you have had when God answered "not yet" to your repeated prayers?

2. Read again Acts 12:12-15. Have you ever heard reports of answered prayer that you found hard to believe? In your opinion, why is it sometimes so difficult for us to believe that God is answering our prayers?

3. What do you think of the following statement in this chapter? "God wants to do great things in India. He wants to do great things in us. He is just waiting for us to ask Him."

CHAPTER 8:
Living Beyond Opposition

God has always been mobilizing His people to share in His mission. Jesus taught and equipped His disciples to follow His example of bearing the cross by taking up their own cross and following Him (Luke 14:27). Jesus called His followers to do as He did, to "Go and make disciples of all nations" (Matthew 28:19). Just before He ascended into Heaven, He declared, "But you will receive power when the Holy Spirit comes on you; and you will be my witness…" (Acts 1:8). Shortly after this promise, the Holy Spirit came upon them and they began the work of mobilizing the people of God into the mission of God. As they were faithful and fruitful, they encountered all kinds of opposition and persecution. Scripture is full of examples of this reality: abuse, imprisonment, and even martyrdom. But we need to keep Ephesians 6:12 in the forefront of our minds: "For our struggle is not against flesh and blood, but against the rulers, against the authorities, against the powers of this dark world and against the spiritual forces of evil in the heavenly realms."

Two things seem to go together: the act of bearing witness to

Christ, and opposition to this witness. When these two things happened in the book of Acts, the results were amazing.

The Apostle Paul explains this connection in Colossians 4:2-6: "Devote yourselves to prayer, being watchful and thankful. And pray for us, too, that God may open a door for our message, so that we may proclaim the mystery of Christ, for which I am in chains. Pray that I may proclaim it clearly, as I should. Be wise in the way you act toward outsiders; make the most of every opportunity. Let your conversation be always full of grace, seasoned with salt, so that you may know how to answer everyone."

For Paul and the early Church, *knowing* the Gospel always resulted in *proclaiming* the Gospel. Possession of faith automatically led to *proclamation* of the faith. This is why, in Colossians 4:2-6, Paul is pleading with the Colossians to pray for him because his imprisonment is keeping him from sharing the Gospel at the scale that God has called him to proclaim it.

It should be like that for us, too, when we grasp the incredible Good News of Christ's resurrection. When we have trusted the living Savior — the one given all authority at God's right hand — how can we keep that Good News to ourselves? To do nothing is not an act of faith. There's no such thing as a privatized faith when it comes to the work of Christ! The Good News is a truth meant to be shared everywhere.

But this is how that is playing out in our lifetime: multitudes of professing Christians say, "I believe that Jesus has saved me and His teaching works for me. But who am I to tell my neighbor, my coworker, my friend what they should believe or not believe? Even more, who am I to tell a stranger or those living in foreign nations what they are to believe?"

I can relate to that.

I remember talking with someone about Mission India's vision to transform India for Christ. That person looked at me and, after a long pause, asked, "Who are we, as Christians, to tell them that what they now believe isn't true, that all their gods are false? Does that not feel extremely arrogant? To claim that a billion Hindus, Sikhs, Buddhists, and Muslims have got it all wrong?" I thought about this and responded by saying, "That would be extremely arrogant, if it wasn't true!"

But if Jesus *did* rise from the dead, if Jesus alone has conquered sin and death, and if Jesus *does* live by the power of God and offers eternal life to all who trust in Him, … it makes perfect sense to tell people those facts. In fact, it would be the height of arrogance *not* to share a truth that you yourself have discovered when that truth invites you into the Kingdom of God.

When we trust in this Savior and believe this Good News, it's so good that we just have to speak about it. The Spirit that lives in us compels us to share it. It all goes back to Jesus when He said in Acts 1:8, "But you will receive power when the Holy Spirit comes on you; and you will be my witnesses…" starting in your own neighborhood and going all the way to the ends of the earth — all the way to India.

This brings us to the second part of Paul's lesson. In Colossians 4:3, Paul says, "And pray for us, too, that God may open a door for our message, so that we may proclaim the mystery of Christ, *for which I am in chains*" (italics mine).

Paul's zeal and passion to proclaim the Gospel has resulted in his being beaten and imprisoned. Persecution is part of the package. Hundreds of millions of people will live their lives never hearing the Good News; and millions more are suffering because of the Gospel.

Knowing the Gospel means proclaiming the Gospel, and proclaiming the Gospel despite opposition to the Gospel.

Why is Paul in chains? Because he proclaimed, "the mystery of Christ." Persecution of those who proclaim the Gospel is the spiritual reality that permeates the stories of the New Testament, the subsequent history of the Church, and even our current world.

This is certainly true in India. I will never forget the story of a woman named Wimal and her family, who came to faith in Christ after hearing the Gospel from a Church Planter named Etasa. When they did so, their entire village turned hostile toward them. Wimal shares their experience: "We had no rations, no electricity, no water, and even the shopkeepers wouldn't allow us to buy anything from them." At night, villagers threw dead dogs, snakes, and stones on their house. Yet Wimal and her family were not willing to abandon their faith in Christ, and they prayed to God for protection.

The family began to meet with Etasa in another village. There, they listened to the Church Planter speak about the Gospel, and his entire congregation prayed for their protection. Praise God for this encouragement for Wimal and her family as they endured such suffering!

After three months, the elders of the village held another meeting and decided to allow Wimal's family to be supplied with electricity and the other rations again. Wimal and her family saw this as a miracle from Jesus. Meanwhile, the villagers wondered how the family could withstand the pressure and follow Christ despite all of the restrictions. They were amazed that the family's needs were still met. Wimal shares, "We could bear all this for Christ's sake."

Wimal's experience is not unusual. What is operating here is what I like to call the Law of Spiritual Momentum. Remember Newton's Third Law of Motion? The idea that for every action (force), there is an equal and opposite reaction (force). Forces are always found in pairs. It's a matter of symmetry. Acting forces encounter other forces in the opposite direction. Think about sitting in a chair. Your body exerts a force downward and that chair needs to exert an equal force upward. If the upward force is not sufficient, you and the chair will collapse onto the floor.

The momentum caused by Wimal's discovery of the great gift of salvation in Christ was met with great opposition. The Law of Spiritual Momentum was operating in the life of Paul, too, as described in his statement to the Colossians. The momentum of proclaiming Good News to the captives stirred up a force of great opposition. In Paul's case, the opposing force manifested itself in beatings and imprisonment, among other things.

This is why Jesus warned, "I am sending you out like sheep among wolves" (Matthew 10:16). If you are a sheep surrounded by wolves, you're in a very vulnerable, scary place. This is why Jesus also said repeatedly, "So don't be afraid" (Matthew 10:31, and many other places). The same God who raised Jesus from the dead is the God who defends the sheep from the wolves and works everything out for their good and for His glory.

Persecution is something with which Indian Christians have always dealt. But now that the Good News is being proclaimed as never before, there is great spiritual momentum leading to fantastic numbers of new believers and new churches. The Law of Spiritual Momentum means that persecution will also increase. And, so it is.

Many people in India — including powerful people in

government, politics, and law enforcement — view Indian Christians as outsiders. One prominent Hindu group has even declared that churches should be eradicated from India altogether. Churches are attacked, believers are beaten, evangelistic workers are falsely accused and imprisoned, Bibles are burned, pastors are threatened, children and families are intimidated. Christian leaders have been beaten to death. Some tribal believers are denied access to water, such as in Wimal's case. Many who receive Christ are expelled, cut off from their communities, and even forced to move out of the village where their ancestors have lived for generations. In some cases, relatives have even tried to kill family members who have become Christians.

There is also the threat of hostile legal action, sometimes forcing the closures of Christian organizations. We recognize how God has blessed Mission India with incredible leaders, board members, and advisors. Since its inception, Mission India has been very intentional about creating strategies and systems that protect the work that God has entrusted to us.

Today, India is arguably the country that is the most responsive to the Gospel in the entire world. Indian Christians in India also experience some of the worst persecution. In 2019, Open Doors USA ranked India tenth on its World Watch List, a list which ranks countries where Christians experience the most severe persecution. That placed India higher than Syria, Nigeria, Iraq, and Saudi Arabia.

The Apostle Paul was the most prominent evangelist in the New Testament Church. He was also the most persecuted. He wrote, "...I have worked much harder, been in prison more frequently, been flogged more severely, and been exposed to death again and again. Five times I received from the Jews the forty lashes minus one. Three times I was beaten with rods, once I was pelted with stones, three times I was shipwrecked, I spent a night and a day in the open sea, I have been constantly on the move. I have been in danger from rivers, in danger from bandits, in danger from my fellow Jews, in danger from Gentiles; in danger in the city, in danger in the country, in danger at sea; and in danger from false believers. I have labored and toiled and have often gone without sleep; I have known hunger and thirst and have often gone without food; I have been cold and naked" (II Corinthians 11:23-27).

Paul's trials were a direct result of proclaiming the Gospel in Asia. Since the Law of Spiritual Momentum tells us that persecution follows proclamation, the question some ask is, "Then, why go? Why take that risk?"

The answer is: Because the power of the Gospel is always greater than the power of the enemy. Colossians 2:15 says, "And having disarmed the powers and authorities, he made a public spectacle of them, triumphing over them by the cross." Can you imagine playing someone in tennis or golf and saying, "I made a spectacle of them" or "I completely disarmed them"? The gift of the Holy Spirit and the reign of Christ guarantee that the power is ours. The Good News includes this promise, that proclaimers will have the power to persevere in the face of persecution. This is why Paul ended his plea to the Colossians: "Pray that I may proclaim it clearly, as I should" (4:4).

Experiences like Paul's are happening all over India. During one visit to India, I was listening to a young man named Moses explain what had happened to him:

"It was at a training program in Karnataka. There were 120 participants. On the second day, around 11:30 at night, anti-Christian activists barged inside our training hall and demanded that the trainers and trainees give them money. When the people refused, they were attacked. Their shoes and mobile phones were taken away from them. As soon as I arrived at the training hall, thirty anti-Christian activists came at us. They pounded us black and blue. Then, they took our bags and emptied them onto the ground — training materials, Bibles, personal items — and burned everything right in front of us. They used abusive language when they spoke and tried to provoke us. They wanted us to react. But God gave us the patience to endure those sufferings. When the police arrived, eight of us were arrested and put in the jail for three days. After our release on bail, we had to return to the police station every month, sign for the attendance, and then attend the court case. (This requires three days of travel for most of us.) And every month, the case got postponed."

For nine long years, I prayed for a resolution to this court case. In 2018, the case was finally dismissed! Sadly, two of the eight partners passed away during the period of trial. But I praise God that, for the six remaining, the long wait finally ended.

When I asked Moses what it was like in prison he said, "Todd, we rejoice that God put us in a place where there were so many people who wanted to hear the Gospel." I was in awe of his faith and passion to make Christ known and also his understanding that opposition is just part of the package.

There are many signs that the rapid growth of the Church in India is sparking ramped-up persecution. Eight Indian states have passed anti-conversion laws, threatening fines and imprisonment for those who leave Hinduism to follow Jesus. The India Parliament is now controlled by a political party that dreams of making India a Hindu nation, having authority over all "outside" religions. The current prime minister is a card-carrying member of the Hindu nationalist group that is behind virtually all anti-Christian persecution in India. The governments of more than half of India's twenty-nine states are also controlled by this radical political party.

The Indian state of Rajasthan has outlawed house churches. Some villages in northern India post signs that declare "No Christians Allowed." Most government officials do not publicly advocate for violence. But officials are often reluctant to prosecute those who attack believers. This has the effect of encouraging thousands of violent acts against Christians.

Just a few steps from another ministry partner in India, a radical Hindu organization has started a youth training center. Their goal is to make India 100 percent Hindu. They are training thousands of young boys and girls to identify and report on Christian activity as spies, and then, to march as paramilitary groups, wielding clubs and threats against Christians.

In the midst of all of these trials, Indian Christians are bolder than ever. Children's Bible Club leaders, Adult Literacy teachers, and Church Planters just won't quit, regardless of the dangers. I recently heard a report on the state of persecution that lasted for fifteen minutes and did not spare any detail of the hate being committed against believers. When the report was finished, you could have heard a pin drop. Finally, the silence broke when the gentleman who gave the report said, "Sir, I am happy to also report that not one of our ministry partners has quit the work." Glory be to God! The perseverance of our brothers and sisters in India, despite so much hardship, is so obvious. You simply can't miss it.

When the Apostle Paul referred to his own suffering, he asked his Christian friends to be watchful, to be thankful, and to pray, specifically, to pray for him, that the door would be open for him to explain the mystery of Christ. The first work of missions is always prayer. Only by the Holy Spirit's miraculous answers to prayer can believers find the joy that transcends suffering.

Believers in India do this better than most of us. Children in the Bible Clubs learn to pray to Jesus. They go home to teach their parents and siblings how to pray as well. Adults in the Literacy Classes pray for one another and for other needy people in their communities. As a result of the training Church Planters receive, the Bible-based Adult Literacy Classes, and the Children's Bible Clubs, prayer groups are formed, allowing new believers to begin to pray to Jesus even before they have professed their faith in Christ. Nearly every new believer in India can testify to a miraculous answer to prayer. Mission India staff in India and America gather every day to pray. Our first and foremost request to all of our ministry partners is to pray. Such prayers empower the spiritual battles that rage all over India. They are the essential ingredient in the activities of all those who put on the armor of God (Ephesians 6:18-20).

If you are ready to live beyond yourself, and possibly to suffer for it, consider carefully Paul's four instructions on how to pray during a season of opposition:

1. **Pray for yourself.** We all need prayer and we should all ask for prayer. But we should also pray for ourselves. I pray for my own soul first. Not because I am more deserving than others, but because if God doesn't awaken, strengthen, humble, and fill my own soul, then I can't pray effectively for others. So, I plead with the Lord every morning for my own soul's perseverance, purification, and power. I pray for an ongoing filling of the Holy Spirit. I pray for boldness

and wisdom and zeal and passion to make Christ known. Without answers to these prayers, I will not be able to stand firm in the face of opposition.

2. **Pray that God will open a door for our message.** Three other times, Paul used this open-door imagery: Acts 14:27, I Corinthians 16:8-9, and II Corinthians 2:12. The open door seems to be a providential set of circumstances that makes the Gospel powerful and effective. So, when Paul pleads with the Colossians, "Pray for us, too, that God may open a door for our message" he means, when Christians pray, God changes circumstances and attitudes and receptivity to the Word, so that instead of meeting an impenetrable barrier, the Word enters through an open door and becomes unusually effective. So, every time your pastor preaches, pray for an open door. Every time you think about your kids, grandkids, neighbors, friends, or coworkers, pray for an open door through which they can enter into a relationship with Christ. Every time you hear about lost people in India, pray for an open door for whomever will be reaching out to them. The doors often open widest when the opposition is strongest!

3. **Pray that the message of Jesus may be clear.** Paul pleaded for prayer. In other words, not only is there a need for God to open doors, but the message passing through the door needs to be clear and powerful—namely, the mystery of Christ. Christ's opponents seek to muddy the

message, to confuse and bewilder those who receive it. Pray that their strategies will fail.

4. **Be watchful when you pray.** We pray continually while looking boldly at the circumstances that confront us and others. Do not take your eyes off them, even if they seem challenging, dangerous, or threatening. Learn from them, all the while praying into them, and expecting God to answer beyond what we can ask or imagine (Ephesians 3:20).

If you want to live beyond yourself, you need to be prepared for opposition and persecution, and to pray for those who are experiencing it.

Questions for discussion:

1. Read again Colossians 4:2-6. What does this passage suggest about opposition to the Good News?

2. This chapter describes many different ways that believers are persecuted. Which of these would you find to be the most difficult to experience? In your opinion, how can believers today best prepare for persecution?

3. Read again the four instructions for prayer that end this chapter. In your opinion, which of these instructions is the most important? Which do you find to be the most difficult?

CHAPTER 9:
Deep Roots and Lasting Fruit

Psalm 1:1-6 was the first passage that my dad ever had me memorize. In fact, he paid me to do it. I am not sure how he landed on this idea, but the concept was to give us boys ten cents for every verse of Scripture that we memorized. And the first text assigned was Psalm 1. That sixty cents might be one of the best investments my parents ever made. It was the first chapter out of the Bible that I ever recited to my dad. It was also the last Scripture I quoted to my dad as he lay dying, and we were waiting for God to take him Home.

> Blessed is the one
>> who does not walk in step with the wicked
> or stand in the way that sinners take
>> or sit in the company of mockers,
> but whose delight is in the law of the Lord,
>> and who meditates on his law day and night.
> That person is like a tree planted by streams of water,
>> which yields its fruit in season
> and whose leaf does not wither —
>> whatever they do prospers.

Not so the wicked!
>   They are like chaff
>   that the wind blows away.
Therefore the wicked will not stand in the judgment,
>   nor sinners in the assembly of the righteous.
For the Lord watches over the way of the righteous,
>   but the way of the wicked leads to destruction.
>   (Psalm 1:1-6)

Throughout my life, I have often wondered why my parents chose that chapter out of all the chapters in the Bible. As I reflect on my dad's life, I think I have the answer: My father wanted me to be like a tree that is planted by streams of living water. I wish I could make a similar investment in you. I would gladly give you sixty cents to memorize those six verses!

Trees are amazing gifts from God. They are things of beauty. They provide shade for the weary and food for the hungry. Their leaves absorb poison and give us fresh air to breathe. When their roots go deep, they are the strongest of plants. Often, they provide wood for the builder. When I think of a tree, I think of shelter, health, prosperity, stability, and strength. My dad used to say that there are two kinds of people in the world: givers and takers. Trees are givers. No wonder my dad wanted me to be like the tree of Psalm 1!

It's not a coincidence that when I remember my dad, I also see the tree of Psalm 1 in his life. His life was rooted in a relationship with Jesus Christ, created and nurtured by the Word of God. Like the blessed person who is described in Psalm 1, my dad took delight in the Word of God.

I remember so often seeing my mom and dad reading the Bible together. I experienced the strength and love of the Word that poured out of their lives as they prayed for each other and for the mercy and faithfulness of God. I had the privilege of watching my dad grow in his love for the Word. But even more importantly, I had the privilege of watching the Word grow my dad in his ability to love others. He loved my mom, he loved his children, he loved those with whom he worked, and he even loved strangers. He was the most generous person I knew, and he taught his children the lessons of generosity. He lived so far beyond himself in his love for others. So, it's no accident that the second Bible passage that my dad paid me to memorize was 1 Corinthians 13 — the chapter on love. I received $1.30 for that one.

Our own fathers can help us understand the significance of God's fatherly love for His children. 1 John 3:1 says, "See what great love the Father has lavished on us, that we should be called children of God!"

Let me tell you about ten-year-old Monika, who lives in south India. Years ago, her dad spent the majority of his income on alcohol. He would come home and argue with Monika's mom, to the point of beating her. He lost most of his money, causing the family to become homeless.

Monika's situation is so typical in India, and so sad, not only because of her family's brokenness, but also because she had no knowledge of the perfect Father in Heaven. Monika was completely ignorant of a father's love.

Scripture is very clear that God is our Father and we are His children. Jesus taught us to address God as "our Father in heaven." If you read all of Jesus' words in the four Gospels, you will find that He refers to God as "Father" more than 150 times.

This was a revolutionary teaching that changed the world. For most people in the world back then, and for many today, the universe is filled with many gods, each with its sphere of influence over the affairs of human beings. These gods can easily be provoked to jealousy or anger. So, they are to be feared and appeased with sacrifices and behavior that will protect people from harm. Back then, and in many cultures today, including the cultures of India, there is no knowledge of a Father in Heaven. People worship their gods out of fear, not because they have experienced love from their gods.

Into such a situation, Jesus comes and declares that there is one God and He is a loving Father. This loving Father is a perfect comfort for anyone who wants to be His child. He is also the perfect example for every one of us earthly fathers to imitate. Like our Heavenly Father, we need to love our children and provide for them security, and have confidence in who they are and who they might become. In telling us what kind of Father God is, Jesus is also telling us what kind of fathers we should be: (This lesson applies to all readers, not just fathers.)

1. God is a *compassionate* Father. He loved us so much that He sent His only begotten Son, our Lord Jesus, to redeem us. He continues to show us compassion as He blesses us in our daily lives. "Cast all your anxiety on him because he cares for you" (1 Peter 5:7).

2. God is a *consistent* Father. Our Heavenly Father never has a bad day. He is not moody — happy one day and crabby the next. He is infinitely dependable to do what He says and to always be the loving Father He claims to be. "If we are faithless, he remains faithful…" (2 Timothy 2:13).

3. God is a *close* Father. He is not far away and remote but is always close by to each of His children. "…though he is not far from any one of us" (Acts 17:27). "The Lord is close to the brokenhearted and saves those who are crushed in spirit" (Psalm 34:18).

4. God is a *competent* Father. He is able to keep His promises. "Now to him who is able to do immeasurably more than all we ask or imagine, according to his power that is at work within us" (Ephesians 3:20).

Those who come to know Jesus begin to experience the loving

compassion of this incredible Father. It's just what Monika needed. Right when she thought life couldn't get any worse, Monika was invited to attend a Children's Bible Club in her neighborhood. Her mom agreed to let Monika attend, but didn't tell her husband, knowing his violent tendencies.

In the Bible Club, Monika sang songs, played games, received help with her schoolwork, and heard Bible stories. She learned about the love of Jesus and was taught how to pray to Him. Monika began praying for her dad, and the other Bible Club members joined her. She started going to church and was motivated by the words found in 1 Corinthians 16:13-14, "... stand firm in the faith; be courageous; be strong. Do everything in love."

When Monika's dad found out that she was attending church, he grew angry and made a plan to beat her in front of everyone at church. But when he arrived at the church with his violent agenda in mind, he froze and instead listened to the pastor. Right in that moment, Jesus answered Monika's prayer and changed her dad's heart.

The drinking stopped; the beatings stopped. Soon he started a business to pay back his debts. Monika's family was made whole again. They finally have love, joy, and laughter because they now know who God the Father is, and that the Heavenly Father has given them His Son who provides a stream of living water to sustain them, nourish them, and give them eternal life. Like the tree of Psalm 1, they are sinking their roots deep into that living water. The tree is bearing fruit. Like a fruitful tree, Monika's father is no longer a "taker" but a "giver." Monika's own earthly father is gradually becoming more and more like her Heavenly Father.

Whether you are a parent trying to follow God's heavenly example or a child looking to spread God's fatherly love, opportunities abound to start giving rather than taking. Monika, her father, and her entire family came to faith in Christ because someone cared enough to make the effort to give them the Good News about Jesus. Some believers were so deeply rooted in Christ and were living so far beyond themselves that they saw the opportunity to extend hope to the other side of the world, and that investment eventually impacted Monika's life and transformed her entire family.

Too many Christians don't understand this dynamic. Their lives are not deeply rooted and, therefore, their tree is not bearing fruit. There is a shallowness in many Christian lives that is encouraged by what Kenda Creasy Dean, in her book *Almost Christian*, calls "diner theology."[8] A diner theology is focused entirely on one's own appetites. It is easy to digest and demands little more than being nice to one another, avoiding interpersonal pain, and saving God for emergencies when necessary. With such faith, one can go about the business of life with little effort or concern for those beyond oneself and one's own family, much less with concern for God. Such shallow living endangers people into becoming the "chaff that the wind blows away" (Psalm 1:4).

The great philosopher, Søren Kierkegaard, illustrates this truth about Scripture in a story about the Prince of Grenada, the heir to the Spanish crown. The prince had been sentenced to life in solitary confinement in Madrid's infamous ancient prison, The Place of the Skull. The fearful, dirty, and dreary nature of the place earned it that name.

Everyone knew that once you entered The Place of the Skull, you did not come out alive. The prince was given one book to read during his entire imprisonment. That book was the Bible. With only one book to read, he read it over and over, hundreds of times. The Bible became his constant companion

After thirty-three years of imprisonment, the prince died. When they came to clean out his cell, they found some notes he had written. Using nails to mark the soft stones of the prison walls, the prince wrote the following notations:

- Psalm 118:8 is the middle verse of the Bible

- Ezra 7:2 contains all the letters of the alphabet except the letter J

- The 9th verse of the book of Esther is the longest verse in the Bible

- No word or name containing more than six syllables can be found in the Bible

How sad for someone to spend the last thirty-three years of his life studying the greatest book of all time, and all he got out of it was trivial information. I am sure he must have loved the book. It helped him pass the time. But it didn't impact his life.

On the other hand, Ravi — who I met during a trip to India — saw his life change because of the Bible. The Changlang district of India's state of Arunachal Pradesh is the definition of the word *remote*. When I asked my new friend, Ravi, how he ended up in this area, he answered by drawing on the history of this district.

"My people were some of the last to hear the Gospel. Nobody travels to Changlang district, and nobody goes to where the Tangsa people live. But, about fifty years ago, or maybe it was more than that, an army man was wandering through the jungle. When the people helped him, he left a Hindi Bible. But no one could read Hindi. Though it was a nice-looking book, they did not know what it said. So, they put it in someone's house and forgot about it.

"Some time later, a fire burned that house to the ground. It was a bamboo house. It burned very hot and very complete. There was nothing left. But when they searched the ashes, they found this book, this paper book, unburned.

"People were shocked and gave the book great honor, though

they still couldn't read it. Then, some years later, a refugee from Myanmar came to the village. When they showed him the book, he told them that it was a Bible. He couldn't read it either. So, some of the people went down to Assam to find someone who could read it to them. When they heard the stories of Jesus, they decided to believe his book and they were baptized.

"They brought the book back to Changlang. But when they started telling what they had learned about Jesus, they were thrown into prison for more than a year. That did not stop them. Now, the people in my district are more than 60 percent Christian."

When you're saturating your mind and heart in the Word of God, with an openness to the presence of Jesus, there's something alive and organic that happens. Something transformational takes place. As the Word becomes a part of you, your life bears fruit (Psalm 1:3).

The Founder of Mission India, John DeVries, was fond of teaching that Scripture is alive, a seed that, when planted, produces the fruit of faith and good works in human lives. Thousands are experiencing the fulfillment of Jesus' promise in John 15:16: "...I chose you and appointed you so that you might go and bear fruit — fruit that will last..."

Your own tree that is deeply rooted can bear much fruit, fruit that reproduces many more trees that will be deeply rooted in Jesus.

If you want to live beyond yourself, sink your roots deep into the Word of God. The best way to truly connect to the love of our Father in Heaven is to connect to the Word that our Father has given us. The Word of God has the power to transform the most selfish, unloving person into the image of Christ. The Living Word of God can change you from living for yourself to living for others.

Questions for discussion:

1. What does it mean for someone to be "like a tree planted by streams of water"? Read Psalm 1 and describe how you could be like that tree.

2. How does Monika's story illustrate the power of God's Word?

3. How has the power of God's Word blessed you and your family? How could you become "more deeply rooted" in the Word of God?

CHAPTER 10:
Dreaming God's Dreams

Not long ago, I almost lost sight of the power of God. I almost lost sight of God's promise to bring salvation to anyone who trusts Him. I learned that there will still be moments of discouragement along the way.

I had reached the point where I had been to India more than twenty times and I just didn't think I could experience anything new in terms of a spiritual challenge. I was pretty sure I had seen it all and heard it all. But then, I went with a friend of mine to deliver audio Bibles to orphans. I began to have my eyes reopened to God's dreams for India. In total, we distributed audio Bibles to about 225 orphans living in a city in southern India.

Before I describe why this experience had such an impact on my life, I should remind you that our youngest daughter, Jori, was an orphan for two years in Kolkata. Through the miracle of answered prayers, Jori came into our forever family. So, you can understand that Indian orphans hold a special place in my heart.

The kids that we met that day ranged in age from four to

sixteen. Every one of them wanted to talk to us, touch us, laugh with us, and be photographed with us. I fell in love with them. I was amazed to see how excited the kids were to receive the Word of God. You would think that they were opening their best Christmas present ever.

But then, I was hit hard when I started asking questions about the orphanage. I was suddenly brought back to the reality of the role of sin in the lives of these sweet, vulnerable children. I was told that the majority of these children had been born to Hindu temple prostitutes and most were HIV positive. These children were either abandoned by their mothers or they had been orphaned by HIV/AIDS.

I could not believe it. I was heartbroken over the way these innocent kids had been affected — infected — by such wickedness around them. I just couldn't get over the fact that, in this day and age, there are women who are serving as temple prostitutes (known as *devadasis* in India). They serve their gods by giving their bodies to be used by men as they believe that, through sexual favors, they are pleasing and worshipping their gods. In some cases, girls begin their careers as temple prostitutes as young as the age of twelve.

It made me so angry. I was overwhelmed and frustrated by the power of darkness which wreaks havoc in the innocent lives of young mothers and little children.

Then I remembered that God gets angry, too. Romans 1:18 reminds us that the wickedness of fallen people breaks God's heart and brings forth God's wrath. What does such wickedness do to you, to me, to the Church of Christ? How do we react to the wickedness unleashed in our world?

Sometimes, as Christians, we like to jump past those verses about the wrath of God to get to the good parts. They tend to make us uncomfortable. After all, our God is a God of love, right? But I think we need to pause to hear the Word of God here. How can we come to terms with the wrath of God? How can we talk about God, without embarrassment, in a way that honors who He really is, and gets past the fact that most of us don't like to think about God's wrath? God is not embarrassed about this.

God's wrath is not the out-of-control anger or vengeance that can characterize human anger. It's a righteous indignation. J. I. Packer describes it this way in his book, *Knowing God*: "God's steady, unrelenting, unremitting, uncompromising antagonism to evil in all its forms and manifestations."[9]

What I did not realize at first was that Hinduism, in all of its various forms, is not so much a religion as it is a way of life. The supreme being, Brahman, with millions of avatars, is only one of the millions of gods many Indians claim. These gods form part of the system called *dharma* — that is, the "right way of living." The gods define *dharma*. They are believed to be always watching, expecting your devotion, demanding your sacrifices, and judging your rituals. Your *karma* is your actions and their appropriate reactions. There is no escaping it. If you try to escape and live a better life, your next *karma* will be a life of even more suffering than this one. That is because everyone participates in the cycle of life-death-rebirth, which is "reincarnation." In Hinduism, the sins or good deeds of your past life determine the horrible or pleasant status of your present life.

So, it's all up to you. Accept your *karma* (your station in life) no matter how miserable, and hope for a better situation in the next life. And if you are suffering now, you are paying for the sins you committed in your past life.

A woman named Sarita was a *devadasi* (a temple prostitute). She was dedicated to the lifelong service of the Yellamma cult in Karnataka, which is where I met her. *Devadasis* serve their goddess by collecting gifts on her behalf and providing services to her devotees. These services include dancing and singing, and, once they reach puberty, sexual favors. Even though the practice has been outlawed in all of India since 1988, governments in two states admit that there are at least fifty thousand practicing *devadasis*, found mostly in rural villages and temples.

Around the time that Sarita turned fourteen, her grandmother declared that she must be dedicated as a *devadasi* to

Yellamma. At the temple, she was given over to a priest who conducted a short and secret ceremony. The priest marked her with a swipe of turmeric powder across her forehead and tied a necklace of red and white beads around her neck as a symbol of her "marriage" to the deity. After returning home, Sarita began her work. Every Tuesday and Friday, she would walk from house to house through her village. She would collect money on behalf of the temple, and, in exchange, would offer herself to the man of the house.

This was Sarita's life for more than twenty years. She bore children, and her daughters were destined for the same horrible life.

Theologian N.T. Wright reminds us that to the oppressed and marginalized people of our planet, to the victims of godlessness and wickedness, God's wrath is good news. Not enough people are angry about the HIV-infected children of temple prostitutes. That is what motivates so many indigenous Christians in India in the work that God has called them to do. They strive, by the power of the Gospel, to eliminate the reasons for God's wrath. They seek to become God's agents to transform lives, today and forever.

Christians step into this worldview of hopelessness with the Good News of grace, forgiveness, love, transformation, and the desire of God to bless every person who comes to Him. Devadasis who come to know Jesus get help from other

Christians, sometimes attorneys, so that they can escape their dismal existence. But, in the meantime, the overwhelming majority of devadasis and their children live lives of utter hopelessness.

Sometimes, we hear such horror stories that we wonder if the darkness is greater than the Gospel. What I needed to see that day as I stood in the orphanage full of prostitutes' children was that the terrible situation was not hopeless. For Paul, the wickedness of terrible situations created a huge urgency, because the Gospel has the power to replace God's wrath with God's love. In the same chapter of Romans, he writes that the Gospel has the power to save *everyone* who believes (Romans 1:16). The Gospel has the power to save temple prostitutes and HIV-infected children. It can transform individual lives. The Gospel also has the power to transform whole families, villages, cities, and even nations. Nothing can resist the Gospel's power.

Two days after visiting those orphans, I was still trying to process what the Spirit was saying to me through that encounter. I was traveling with one of our Indian partners in the state of Karnataka and I shared how upset I was about those children. He listened politely, and then a big smile came over his face. I asked him, "Why are you smiling?"

He told me that Mission India had just launched a training program for a Church Planter whose calling from God was to reach devadasis. In addition to that, Adult Literacy Classes had succeeded in bringing hundreds of prostitutes to know Christ and these classes were now becoming outreach points of the church he was planting. He said, "I have no doubt that over the next year, many more temple prostitutes will begin to follow Christ."

As I listened to his confidence in the power of the Gospel, I realized that the Holy Spirit was, once again, so far ahead of me in transforming India for Christ. I praise God that the Holy Spirit gave me clarity to see that — regardless of the wickedness of seemingly hopeless situations — the righteousness of God can be revealed through the simple obedience of God's people. I praise God that I was able to be a part of that righteousness in delivering Scriptures and sharing the hope of Jesus Christ with those precious children. I pray that our righteous God will raise up from those children mighty evangelists who will eradicate the evil work of Satan. I pray that Christ and His Kingdom will shine the light of salvation into the darkest places of India.

Mission India, at its heart, is a church-planting ministry. We know that when a new gathering of Spirit-filled believers begins to meet for the first time, the entire surrounding community is bathed in the light of Christ's presence. This is God's dream for India: Saturating India with the light of the Gospel so that Christ becomes visible in every village and within reach of every person.

Indian Christians are already bringing so much light in the

midst of so much darkness; I am proud to be able to partner with them and do what Paul calls "living out the faith, living out the Gospel." Such faith is so compelling that people will *want* to hear about it. This is why Paul begins his letter to Rome by reminding the Roman believers that "[Their] faith is being reported all over the world" (Romans 1:8). Paul traveled widely, and he is saying, "Everywhere I go, all over the world, people talk about your faith, your gift for making Christ known, your hard work, your obedience," so much so that Paul is confident that "the God of peace will soon crush Satan under your feet" (Romans 16:20).

Think about this. Some churches are famous for the size of their membership. Some churches are famous for their architecture, their buildings, their stained-glass windows. Some churches are famous for the teachings of their pastor. Some churches are famous for their music. But are these things the content of God's dreams for His fallen world? How many are famous for their faith? For their obedience to the Gospel? For the debt of love that propels them into the lives of the lost? How many are famous for the power to transform lives once lost in the abyss of wickedness?

What do our churches in North America *want* to be known for? Does the urgency to make disciples of all nations show itself in our actions, our giving, or our priorities for ministry? Do we really believe that God's dream — to establish a worshipping fellowship of believers in every community — could actually come true?

How are we doing? To illustrate this, let's suppose that we are all statistically the average North American Christian. We are earning several thousands of dollars each month. Let's calculate for each $1,000 that we earn, how much of that $1,000 we are giving away as our donation to worthy causes. Well, research tells us that we are giving away $24 out of every $1,000, or an average of 2.4% of our income.

Now, of that $24, how much are we giving to fulfill God's dream to bring the Gospel to those people in foreign countries rather than our own communities? How far are we living beyond ourselves? Researchers say that out of every $24 donated, $1.20 goes overseas and $22.80 stays in the United States.

Of our $1.20 that goes overseas, how much will be directed toward people who are unreached by the Gospel, those who need to hear it for the first time? 12 cents. Just 12 cents will go to reach the unreached people groups in our world.

India contains nearly half of all the unreached people groups in the world and yet of that 12 cents, only about 2 pennies will make it to India, the most unreached nation on the planet! Out of $1,000 … 2 cents. Do you know what I do when I get back 2 cents in change? Leave it behind. I don't even want to bother with it.

Somehow, we have allowed a serious disconnect to develop

between God's dream to transform our broken world and our commitment to God's agenda. How can we begin to dream God's dreams and get in step with God's agenda for the world?

Sometimes, the dream can feel so big and the disconnect so wide that we don't know where to start! Here's one idea: Jean and I pray for India all the time. But how do you pray for 1.3 billion different lives? In all honesty, we pray really hard for one person in particular. She is someone we are so grateful for. She is the woman, unknown to us, who brought our precious daughter, Jori, into this world.

When we brought Jori home from India, I was not yet working for Mission India. We talked about so many things that we were hoping God would do in her life, things like bonding with Jean and me, as well as our other children. We prayed for her to learn English, to like American food, and to want to join not only our family but also her new "forever family" in the Kingdom of God.

But one of our prayers for Jori went way beyond us. We prayed that Jori would meet her birth mom in Heaven someday. So, Jean and I began praying that God would bring Jori's birth mom into a relationship with Jesus Christ. We didn't know where she was. We didn't know anything about her. We had never met her, and probably never would. And we didn't know how God would do it.

Fast forward eighteen months. I had just joined Mission India, and Jean and I were sitting in our family room watching TV. All of a sudden, Jean reached over and hit me on the arm and said, "Todd, I just had the most amazing thought! Wouldn't it be amazing if Jori's birth mom came to know Jesus Christ through the ministry of Mission India? Maybe through a church that is planted in her village or neighborhood? Or through an Adult Literacy Class that she is invited to attend? Or, perhaps, Jori has a sibling we know nothing about, and that boy or girl ends up in a Children's Bible Club where he or she would learn about Jesus and share Christ with his or her mother? Wouldn't that be an incredible answer to our prayers?"

We are ready to be surprised by God. We want to keep living beyond our own little family. We are convinced that you can dream God's dreams — even when they seem impossible, or nebulous, or so unlikely — and God will give you a way to contribute to their fulfillment. The secret is to know what it is that God dreams, and to look for ways to make those dreams your own.

When we think about our own world, we should remember the map located near the back of this book! This map is like a giant advertising billboard: Look there! Look where you can pay your debt of love to the unreached! See the places where you can begin to dream God's dream to connect Jesus to all of those people who need His offer of eternal life.

God dreams the impossible. When we commit ourselves to

God's dreams, we learn why all things are possible with Him. When we bring Christ into a person's life, we open the doors to every kind of blessing. When we bring Christ into a community, every other good thing becomes possible.

If you want to live beyond yourself, you need to dream God's dreams. This means not only living beyond yourself, but also living beyond your family, beyond your neighborhood, and even beyond your country.

Questions for discussion:

1. In your own words, how would you describe God's dream for our world? How would you describe God's dream for India?

2. This chapter describes the fact that for every $1,000 in earnings by American believers, only 2 cents is given toward fulfilling God's dream for India. In your opinion, what accounts for this disparity?

3. What kind of people experience God's wrath as "Good News"? How can we begin to dream God's dreams for these people?

CHAPTER 11:
One Whom Jesus Loves

It was six months into our marriage and I was coming home from what had been a glorious day. I'd been out playing basketball for three hours. I thought to myself, "I get to go home to my new wife. She'll fix dinner, we'll have dessert, and then we can hang out."

Well, I walked in the house and said, "Hi Jean, how are you?" And do you know what she said? "I'm fine." Being newly married, I actually believed that Jean meant what she said. I did not know that this phrase was code for "I'm not fine." We dated for almost five years before we were married, so I probably should have! But I didn't.

Anyway, I came in from playing basketball and asked how she was doing, and she responded with, "I'm fine. Let's eat!" We sat down and there was an awkward pause. I picked up on the fact that something was wrong. So, I asked if she was okay. She said, "I said I'm fine. But I do have one question: Is this how we're going to live? I am just wondering if you are going to play basketball every night. I need more time with you." Of course, what I was thinking was, "Huh? We live together. What do you mean you need more time? I am only playing basketball four nights a week and on Saturday afternoons, and you get to come along and cheer for me!"

Eventually I figured things out, thanks in part to *The Five Love Languages* book Jean and I read together. When we were first married, I didn't understand love languages, and it didn't dawn on me that there were different types.[10]

This now-humorous story points me toward a powerful truth that still unleashes unbelievable insight into our lives through one of Jesus' most incredible miracles. The miracle came about because Jesus' friends, Mary and Martha, had this down. They knew exactly what Jesus' love language was!

John 11:1-5 says, "Now a man named Lazarus was sick. He was from Bethany, the village of Mary and her sister Martha. (This Mary, whose brother Lazarus now lay sick, was the same one who poured perfume on the Lord and wiped his feet with her hair.) So the sisters sent word to Jesus, 'Lord, the one you love is sick.' When he heard this, Jesus said, 'This sickness will not end in death. No, it is for God's glory so that God's Son may be glorified through it.' Now Jesus loved Martha and her sister and Lazarus."

Mary and Martha's little brother, Lazarus, is on the doorstep of death. From what they can tell, death is only moments away. Desperate, they know their friend, Jesus, is several miles down the road. They need to get Him to come and save their brother, heal him, and deliver him.

Mary and Martha write a note. The Scripture says, "So the sisters sent word…" (v. 3). They would have written a note and sent a runner to deliver it to Jesus. The contents of this note had to elicit an immediate response from Jesus. They had to grab Jesus' attention, convince Him to drop everything, and come to save their little brother's life.

Think about this: If you had one note to save your brother's life, one note to save your spouse's life, one note to save your loved one's life, what would you write? Maybe you would write, "God, you need to save her! She's one of the good people. She loves you. She's a great sister. She's too young to die."

Mary and Martha write their little note to save Lazarus' life, and it reads: "Lord, the one you love is sick" (v. 3).

It is not, "Lord, behold Lazarus, the one that loves you, the one that serves you, is sick. Would you please come and heal him?" In the heat of the moment, Mary and Martha know that what will get Jesus to come and heal Lazarus is not reminding Jesus of Lazarus' love for Him, but reminding Jesus of *His* love for Lazarus. Everything is based on God's love for us.

John 11:33-36 says, "When Jesus saw her weeping, and the Jews who had come along with her also weeping, he was deeply moved in spirit and troubled. 'Where have you laid him?' he asked. 'Come and see, Lord,' they replied. Jesus wept. Then the Jews said, 'See how he loved him!'"

It's a recurring theme in the New Testament narrative that those closest to Jesus seem far more preoccupied with Jesus' love for them than their love for Him. Mary and Martha are not the only ones who know this. John, the disciple who recorded the miracle of Jesus raising Lazarus from the dead, was one of the three followers that were extra close to Jesus. John is the one who leans close to Jesus at the Last Supper for the most private conversation.

John did something that I find socially awkward: he nicknamed himself. Have you ever had a nickname? The first rule of nicknames is that you don't give them to yourself; others give them to you. But John nicknames himself. What's equally awkward about this is the nickname he chooses for himself. John refers to himself in the third person — also awkward — and he calls himself "the disciple whom Jesus loved."

What arrogance, right? This is not okay! To claim for yourself this special name, implying that you are God's favorite! And not just once, but five times, John gives himself this prideful title. What do we do with that? What did God do with it?

I would like to think that five times God watches as John pens that in his Gospel story. And five times God says, "That's right. I inspired him to name himself that. Leave it in the book." Since then, millions and millions and millions of people have read and heard about "the disciple whom Jesus loved."

Think about your own loved ones: sons, daughters, spouses, and friends. Perhaps you are wondering about them, those brought up in church who have heard about the Savior's love, but, for some reason, have never claimed that love for themselves. How you wish they would say, "I, the one Jesus loves!"

Now, imagine that they are completely unaware of God's love! Never read the Gospel of John, or the story of Lazarus, or are even aware of the idea that human beings can be "the ones God loves"! Instead, their entire world, everything they know, is completely void of this Good News! Their gods are not gods of love. They have no access to a Bible. They have never met a Christian believer, nor ventured by a Christian church, nor heard a Christian broadcast. It's heartbreaking. Imagine what it does to the heart of God.

India has more unreached people than anywhere else on earth. Approximately 85 percent don't even know anyone who is a Christian. The only "love language" Satan has presented them with is *karma*.

These beliefs breed a kind of fatalism and indifference to suffering, especially the suffering of the most helpless members of society. To make matters worse, every Hindu person is born into a certain caste. There are hundreds of castes, and they form a hierarchy of privilege and status. There is no choice regarding a person's caste. The person is born into it, and his or her children will be born into it.

Below the lowest caste, there are those who are not worthy of a caste and, therefore, not considered fully human. The lowest of the low. They are known as *Dalits* ("crushed") or "Untouchables."

One of Mission India's directors was born a Dalit. When she was younger, her parents tied brooms to their waists so that they would drag behind them on the ground. That way, the broom would wipe out their footprints to eliminate the possibility that any person of a higher caste would become polluted by stepping on them. They had to be careful what side of the path to walk on, lest their shadows touch a person of a higher caste.

How ridiculous it would sound for a Dalit person to say that he or she was "the one God loves." And yet, neither would a person from a higher caste be bold enough to say that. More than 330 million gods make demands and requirements of, and threaten, their human worshippers, but they do not show any love.

This is what hundreds of millions of people in India live with day after day after day. God's mission is for someone to tell them the truth: Jesus is calling people of all castes to become the sons and daughters of the Great King. In doing so, He abolishes the very concept of caste. Just as Lazarus and John were known as "the ones Jesus loved," so, too, can any person in India claim that nickname.

The story of Lazarus at Bethany points us to the story of Jesus at Calvary. At Calvary, Jesus shed much more than tears; He shed His blood. Calvary happened not so much to show that we would love Him, but to demonstrate how much He loves us.

Jesus loved so far beyond Himself it defies our imagination. When Jesus rose from the grave, He proved that God is stronger than death. In fact, God is *life*, and death has no power over Him. Christ's death on the cross and His resurrection are a strong demonstration of God's commitment of love to people. His is a love that wins. And just as God's love for individuals is displayed so powerfully in Jesus, so His love wins in the lives of Jesus' followers. This is why it was not until after the resurrection that Jesus gave the commission to His followers to call all people everywhere into the new life that He offers. Look what happens when you love beyond yourself!

However, this doesn't mean that it's easy. Loving others is about proclaiming and demonstrating God's love. The love of God is not something we only *know about*; it is what we *do*. It's absolutely mind-boggling to know that "God so loved the world." In the original language in John 3:16, "world" means "sinful system." Jesus loves people throughout the entire world who are trapped and are part of this sinful system.

I confess, sometimes I have wanted to say, "God, I don't know how to break this news to you, but you are going to get hurt by loving these people, by loving this world. Many of them will never reciprocate. The extraordinary love and sacrifice you have for them might not be returned. You're going to be disappointed. People are just not interested.

I've been there. Perhaps you have, too.

Jesus dealt with this type of doubt in the Lazarus miracle:

> When Mary reached the place where Jesus was and saw him, she fell at his feet and said, "Lord, if you had been here, my brother would not have died." When Jesus saw her weeping, and the Jews who had come along with her also weeping, he was deeply moved in spirit and troubled. "Where have you laid him?" he asked. "Come and see, Lord," they replied. Jesus wept. Then the Jews said, "See how he loved him!" ...
>
> So they took away the stone. Then Jesus looked up and said, "Father, I thank you that you have heard me. I knew that you always hear me, but I said this for the benefit of the people standing here, that they may believe that you sent me." When he had said this, Jesus called in a loud voice, "Lazarus, come out!" The dead man came out, his hands and feet wrapped with strips of linen, and a cloth around his face. Jesus said to them, "Take off the grave

clothes and let him go" (John 11:32-36, 41-44).

Jesus spoke these words into the cave that was Lazarus' tomb: "Lazarus, come out!" Somebody once joked by saying that it's a good thing that Jesus said, "Lazarus" because if He had just said, "Come out," all the dead people would have come forth. That was a specific word, to a specific man, at a specific time.

Jesus waited until the situation was humanly impossible. He did it in His own power. He showed that there was life when all they saw was death. Death did not have the last word. Jesus did; and love prevailed. Jesus still does; and love is still prevailing.

God's best work is not just about us as individual believers. It's usually focused on the Church and the body of believers working together in love to transform people. When Lazarus came stumbling out of his tomb, Jesus turned to his family and friends and said, "Take off the grave clothes and let him go." Jesus is the one who brought Lazarus from death to life. But He calls on the gathering of believers, the Church, to finish what He started by unbinding people.

Trusting God, we are called to help people move from death to life. Believing in the power of Christ's love, we proclaim that love and demonstrate it to others, not only in our own communities, but even on the other side of the world.

A Christian couple did that when they gave generously to support a Children's Bible Club in India. They impacted a middle-aged widow, Punia, who had a son named Bishal. Shortly after Bishal's birth, Punia's husband died. He had been a laborer in a factory.

Punia's backstory is heartbreaking. When he did not return home after work one day, Punia went to the factory to track him down. The people told her, "Your husband fell into the furnace and died." They did not allow her to see the body. They gave her 1,000 rupees (about $14) as compensation and sent her away.

The family of Punia's husband offered no help and gave her no words of love or encouragement. Instead, as often happens in India, they kicked her out of the family. They told her that now that their son was dead, she was no longer a part of the family. With no place to live, she made her way north and found work in a brick factory. The work was excruciating. For eighteen hours of daily, backbreaking labor, she was paid 50 rupees (less than $1), the going wage for brick workers.

Bishal was getting older and it didn't work for Punia to bring him to the brick factory. So, she hit the road again until she ended up where she is today. Punia said, "We had a hard time adjusting and had to sell everything we owned in order to eat." She found work in a tea field that provided enough money to buy food, but not enough to buy utensils to cook it. "So, along with the work in the tea fields, I began begging for money on a train platform. I also did chores and cleaning in people's homes."

She built a small tarp house for their belongings and ended up sleeping on the train platform at night. Young Bishal became depressed and hated his life. But one day, someone invited him to attend a Children's Bible Club. He learned Christian songs, got help with his schoolwork, and, best of all, he began to hear and experience the love of Christ. This was an entirely new experience, since no one besides his mother had ever shown him any love or concern.

As Bishal learned more about the love of Jesus, he shared it all with his mother. Then, one Sunday, he convinced his mom to go to the church service nearby. It was like nothing Punia had ever experienced. Instead of being ignored, she was welcomed. Up until that point, she had always felt despised. But, for the first time in her life, she felt accepted and loved by the church members. Punia soon received Jesus Christ as her Savior.

Punia and Bishal still struggle with poverty today. But when Bishal was injured and had to go to the hospital, it was members of their church who helped with all their needs. When the rains brought floods and washed out their worn-down home, it was members of the church who took them in and helped rebuild their home, replacing tarps with wood. I praise God for the couple who sponsored this Children's Bible Club. I praise God for their prayers and for the partner in India who started the Bible Club in the village into which Punia walked.

There are thousands of similar stories all over India where people are discovering the reality of being the "one whom Jesus loves." Every year through Mission India's programs, at least five million children hear the Gospel. Every year, more than ten thousand new churches are established. Every year, more than two million people in India begin to follow Jesus for the first time. And by loving others beyond themselves, they are transforming families, villages, and cities. We look forward to the day when this love will transform all of India!

Living beyond yourself means loving beyond yourself. When you love beyond yourself, you unleash God's power in unbelievable ways.

Questions for discussion:

1. Which do you think is more important: God's love for you, or your love for God? How does the story of the raising of Lazarus (John 11) help to answer that question? How does the story of Punia and Bishal help to answer that question?

2. List some ways that we, like God, can "love beyond ourselves."

CHAPTER 12:
Beyond Yourself, Miracles Await

I met Deorcus on a trip to Kolkata. To most Indians, she was probably just another poor, untouchable woman. To me, she was unforgettable.

Deorcus was a young, illiterate woman, raised in a devout Hindu family. Wanting to improve her life, she started attending one of Mission India's Adult Literacy Classes, eventually graduating as one of the top students. During her education, she showed a lot of interest in knowing more about Jesus. She confessed that the Hindu gods she was worshipping left her feeling alone and fearful that she could never please them. Wona, her literacy teacher, began calling on her at her home. Her parents became very angry when they discovered that Deorcus was learning about Jesus, so they forbade her from attending the Adult Literacy Class. Without her parents' knowledge, Deorcus continued attending the literacy classes anyway.

One day, Deorcus became very ill. She was living in constant pain. Her parents prayed to their family gods and even brought in a witch doctor who performed various rituals. But Deorcus only got worse. When Wona suggested that Deorcus invite her pastor to come and pray for her, she said yes. The pastor and Wona prayed over her, anointing her with oil, and Deorcus was partially healed! This convinced her that Wona's God might have something more to give her.

So, the next Sunday, Deorcus attended Wona's church. When the invitation was given, she went forward for prayer. During that prayer, a force came over her and she fell to the ground. When she stood up, she could no longer feel the pain of her illness! She was completely healed. At that moment, Deorcus gave her life to Christ. She went home and told her parents that Jesus had healed her, and that He was more powerful than their family gods. Her parents were furious. They threw her out of their house, disowning her and pledging never to speak to her again.

By God's grace, Deorcus was invited to move in with a friend from the church. She found a job and began to save money to get her own place. Deorcus met a Christian man and they eventually married. She continued to attend church, Bible studies, and prayer groups, and was growing in her faith to the point where the pastor asked if she would consider being trained as a Church Planter. She agreed and enrolled in the program.

As part of her training, Deorcus began to evangelize to people. Every morning, Deorcus climbed onto the roof of her house and prayed aloud over the city. The first person she led to Christ was a neighbor, a lady who heard those prayers. I talked to that lady when I was in India and she told me that she had never heard anyone pray for other people with so much love and passion. The neighbor knocked on Deorcus's door one day and asked if she would tell her about this Jesus that she was praying to. Deorcus shared about Christ, and this woman immediately received Jesus as her Savior. She brought her sister to Deorcus and asked her to tell her sister about Jesus, too, and the sister then gave her life to Christ.

In time, a small church formed in Deorcus's village. At the time of my visit, the church was in its fifth month of life. Deorcus had established five prayer groups and had called on 256 families. A total of fifty-seven people had received Christ as their Savior and were now attending her church. I heard many of their testimonies at the service. There is something so powerful about personal testimonies and the joy that comes from them as people share how they were rescued from spiritual darkness and brought into the light of Christ!

During the worship service, I was asked to preach, as is common when foreigners visit Indian churches. I talked about why we worship God. My translator must have added his own words to my message because the people were engaged to a point that I have rarely experienced as a pastor. After my message, we sang a hymn and I gave the blessing. I lifted up my hand and said, "May God bless you and keep you. May He cause His face to shine upon you and be gracious unto you. May He lift up His countenance upon you and give you His peace, so that you can give the peace of Christ to whomever comes in your path."

As I said these last words, a woman in Deorcus's church fell face down on the ground and started shouting. At first, I thought she was overcome by the Holy Spirit. But then, as her words turned to screams, I sensed darkness and evil. They told me that the woman was overcome by a demon. So, we got down on our knees, laid our hands on this woman, and commanded the demon to come out of our sister. I looked intently at the woman and said, "I command you in the name of Jesus to come out of her. And I command you through the power of the resurrection of Jesus to go to the foot of the cross of Jesus Christ to be destroyed forever." My wife, who was with me on the trip, told me later that it was clear to everyone in the room that the woman was instantly at peace through deliverance and the power of prayer.

The woman stood up and began to tell us her story. "For the past year, at different times, while walking here and there, a dark force would come over me. My hands and feet would curl up, and I was thrown face first onto the ground. I would cry out in words that I could not understand. This happened to me over and over, and it happened just now as our worship service was ending. When you prayed for me, the dark force left, and I felt a great peace come over me."

Several American friends, who were with me in the service,

were stunned. The rest of the congregation was calm. They were not alarmed at all and did not even seem surprised. Demonic possession is such a common reality in their lives that they have become accustomed to witnessing the power of Jesus release people from the powers of darkness. They simply and enthusiastically began to praise Jesus for His deliverance and grace. And I? I praised God. I praised Him for the power of His Holy Spirit. I praised Him that, years ago, He had brought a friend into my life who began to disciple and train me in the ministry of healing and deliverance, including the casting out of demonic forces.

God performed this miracle because, years ago, that friend of mine was living beyond himself and invited me into it. His name was Tim. This experience reminded me of a time when Tim and I were attending a healing conference in Chicago. Tim had received a call from a woman who thought she was possessed by demons. He said, "Todd, do you want to come along and pray for her?" I paused and said, "... maybe," which then quickly turned to a "yes."

As Tim and I were driving, he suggested a time of prayer for those of us in the car, specifically, to confess our sins. Tim had had the experience of demons publicly accusing him of various sins. Hesitantly, I told Tim that I thought I understood how to cast out a demon, but I didn't know what to do once it was out. Tim told me to command the demon to go to the foot of the cross of Christ to be destroyed forever, and that's exactly what I remembered to do in Deorcus's church service.

I share this story to tell you how thankful I am for the on-the-job training that Tim had given me as he lived beyond himself. It helped prepare me for Deorcus and the woman possessed by demons. This is why we give on-the-job training to Church Planters in India. Living beyond yourself does not come naturally; you need to practice it. I pray that you will see that this entire story has one central theme: In Ephesians 4:11-12, Paul tells us that Christ Himself "gave the apostles, the prophets, the evangelists, the pastors and teachers, to equip his people for works of service…" When we equip the saints for ministry, we are living way beyond ourselves, and teaching others to do likewise. This is Deorcus's story. It is my story. And it is the foundation and purpose of why we exist as a ministry: To see India transformed by the love of Christ.

The Great Commission is too big for anyone to accomplish alone and too important to not try doing together. I thank God that He has given us a wonderful partnership with Indian believers as we join together with them in the task of reaching India. Prior to Christ (in the Old Testament), the message of the Kingdom was "centripetal" — that is, drawing others *in*. When Christ came, He turned that upside down and made the Gospel "centrifugal" — that is, a power that goes *out*. That is why we equip others. It's the most effective means to impact the darkness.

God is doing this all over India in extraordinary ways. During that same trip to India, I heard more incredible testimonies:

- A Hindu man and his wife heard the Gospel. The wife was saved, but the husband still did not believe. Every morning, they would get up and pray. The husband prayed to his Hindu god and the wife prayed to Jesus Christ. The husband told me, "Guess who won? It was Jesus, and today I am a follower of Him."

- A little girl in a Children's Bible Club received Christ and began to share the Gospel with all her Hindu friends. Her friends' parents became so angry that they forbade their children from playing with her. She told me, "Some of my friends still play with me. They have received Jesus. They just don't dare tell their parents. So, would you pray that they would have courage and I would be able to play with the rest of my friends to tell them about Jesus?"

- An Adult Literacy teacher who works in the Red-Light District of Kolkata is teaching prostitutes to read and write. She told me that she is sharing with them the power of the Kingdom of God. She also gives them home-based business skills so that they can get out of prostitution. She has helped many of them relocate to other areas of the city.

- A man in West Bengal encountered a traumatic experience, which convinced him to give his life to equipping others to share the Gospel. Today, he serves as a professor at a Kolkata university and equips Church Planters to reach middle-class and high-caste Hindus.

These stories are just from one trip to India; they are taking place every single day through our partners who are spreading out over the entire nation of India.

I'm in my fifties and I have never experienced such an extreme contrast between darkness and light as I did during that trip. I visited the Kali Temple, home to the famous goddess, Kali, in Kolkata and saw people waiting in line for five or six hours to make an offering to the deity. Literally next door is Mother Teresa's home for the dying where followers of Jesus devote their entire lives to caring for the terminally ill. As I visited both of these places, I thought Kali's temple should be called the temple of the dying. I asked my Hindu tour guide why people are willing to wait so long to make their offering. He said, "To the right side sit our gods and to the left sit our ancestors. We live life to appease them all so that they do not become displeased with us and pour out their anger upon us. That is why we wait in long lines to bring offerings to them."

Living in fear encourages people to live entirely for themselves, desperate to protect themselves and their families. Living in the freedom of God's love encourages us to live beyond ourselves to impact and equip others to witness His daily miracles in our lives and the lives of those around us.

If you want to learn how to live beyond yourself, you need to learn how God can equip ordinary people to experience extraordinary miracles. Then, you are able to equip others to expand the Kingdom of God.

Questions for discussion:

1. Do most people in your town or city believe in miracles? How about people in your church?

2. Of the several stories of miracles told in this chapter, which do you find to be the most encouraging? Which, if any, did you find hard to believe? Why do you suppose people are so skeptical of stories of miracles?

3. Someone once told me, "It seems that there are more miracles in India than we experience in America." Would you agree? How can living beyond ourselves open our hearts to see and believe God's miracles?

CHAPTER 13:
Greater Than We Could Ever Imagine

I have come to the conclusion, rather reluctantly, that I will never fully comprehend Christ's love for me.

As I've mentioned, the founder of Mission India, John DeVries, cites Ephesians 3:20 as a foundational verse for what God has called us to accomplish in India: "Now to him who is able to do immeasurably more than all we ask or imagine, according to his power that is at work within us..." We receive constant reminders that whatever big prayers we pray for India, God so often does more than we have asked or imagined.

The same passage includes Paul's prayer that God's people will realize "how wide and long and high and deep is the love of Christ, and to know this love that surpasses knowledge..." (Ephesians 3:18-19). This is the Grand Canyon of the Kingdom of God, an expanse of blessings so extensive that no person can fully comprehend the transformation that Christ works in those who trust Him.

This rings true so dramatically for many people who have been transformed by the power of Christ in ways that we never could have predicted. It's not only the individuals, but whole communities that incarnate God's dreams for His image bearers.

During one visit to India, my colleague, Josh, found himself traveling in the tribal belt of southern Rajasthan, the western-most state of India that borders Pakistan. Josh shares, "We had turned off the highway onto a small dirt road and began slowly winding our way back into the hills. Eventually, we ended up at a church in a small village. The pastor greeted us, invited us into his spacious church building, offered us tea, and began to share how God was blessing him and his village.

"During our conversation, I got the sensation that I had met this man before. Somehow, he seemed familiar to me. So, I started asking the pastor questions and finally said, 'Have we ever met before?'

"His name was Karsenbai. He looked at me closely and said, 'Yes, I think maybe we have.'"

Josh had only been to Rajasthan, a state made up of 68.5 million people, once before, seven years prior.

When Josh returned home from that trip, he dug through his old trip notes. Sure enough, he found photos and notes that he had taken seven years earlier. A younger Karsenbai was among a group of Church Planters Josh had interviewed seven years before. He had taken Josh to the village where he had begun his evangelistic work. It was easy to recognize Karsenbai's face in the photos. But, looking at the background and the scenery around him, Josh could not recognize anything else.

The village in the old photos was a very different place than the village he visited. Josh remembered a long, hot walk to get to the village. There was no road back then. So, he had trudged up and down those barren hills on a dusty footpath with the blazing sun beating down upon him.

In that village of long ago, Josh had found a small building, perhaps five hundred square feet, that was serving as Karsenbai's home. It doubled as a place of worship. Josh worshipped with a dozen new believers packed into this tiny structure. He remembers being struck by two contradictory thoughts: How great it was to see the first fruits of the Gospel, and how difficult it was to imagine the life of a Church Planter in a place so desolate that you had to walk for an hour to get there. And when you arrived, it was not the kind of place where anyone would want to live.

Fast forward seven years. Karsenbai's worship building is now an impressive, concrete structure where sixty families gather every Sunday, where children gather for Sunday school, where meetings for prayer and Bible study minister to the village residents.

Five nights a week, Karsenbai offers the use of the church veranda for an Adult Literacy Class where thirty illiterate men and women are learning how to read and write. One of his church members is the teacher. It's an outreach program and many of the students have already professed Christ. They will soon join the church.

Not only is the church growing, but the village, too, is being transformed: No more long hikes to get to the village from the main highway. Over the last two years, God answered prayers for a new road graded into the hillside, with much of the cost donated and work done by the church members. Once the road was completed, electricity soon followed — a revolutionary development for these rural villagers.

As God loves to bless people, it is in His heart and mind to transform individuals, families, and entire communities, bringing them not only roads and electric power, but so much more. He will bring a fullness of life: physical, spiritual, and social transformation that is more than they imagined. When you bring the Lord Jesus Christ to a place, all the other blessings of the Kingdom of God will follow. Josh summarizes his story by saying, "When you bring Jesus, Jesus brings everything else."

How do you measure that? How do you measure what the Holy Spirit does through the years that follow our evangelistic investments of time and resources? Every year, a team at Mission India adds up our ministry results. But we also have learned to trust God to come alongside and start *multiplying* blessings in ways that are beyond our ability to plan or imagine! Stories like

Karsenbai's continue to unfold all over India!

Imagine with me an eight-year-old boy from a poor village. His background is classified as low caste, the son of a man known to be a communist agitator, a man described by those who know him as a "rough character."

One summer morning, this little boy is walking through the village and he passes by a building. He hears laughing and singing. So, he approaches it to get a closer look. Peering in through a window, he sees that the building is full of kids, many of them his own age. They are playing games, singing songs, and having a great time. He has never experienced anything like that, and he becomes jealous.

So, the next morning, he goes back and he finds the kids outside playing games. Just then, an adult calls out to them and the children start lining up by height in order to file back into the building, shortest at the front and tallest at the back. That is when this little boy sees his opportunity. He builds up his courage and jumps in line in just the right spot. Filing in with the group, he spends the rest of the day in there — and he loves it. The leaders undoubtedly notice the newcomer and they are fine with it. So, the little boy goes back every day to the Baptist church where he is singing happy songs about a man named Jesus, playing games, and hearing stories that are so interesting and so different from anything he has heard before.

A week later, the children have been called together for their final meeting, and their teacher explains that Jesus is calling each one of them to put his or her trust in Him, to learn from Him, and to follow His teaching in his or her daily lives. The boy walks forward with several other children and prays a pledge to love and follow Christ.

Now, picture with me a little girl born to a desperately poor *Dalit* ("Untouchable") family in a small village. A village so cursed, its name means "empty place." The village is full of poor people. But as *Dalits*, the girl's family members are the poorest of the poor and despised by all the other villagers. She is the fourth daughter born into this poor family. There is not enough to eat, and this little girl is seen as such a devastating burden that her grandmother prays to the gods for her to die.

Her mother is illiterate and her father dies when she is only four years old. But before he dies, her father finds work as a translator for a missionary. Hearing the Good News over and over, he soon becomes a Christian. Upon his death, he leaves his family no earthly legacy, no savings, no property, only the dire prospect of an indigent widow trying to survive with too many children. But he does leave his young daughter with a legacy of faith and hope.

What do you think God can do with two children like that? The eight-year-old son of a communist? Or, the unwanted fourth daughter of an untouchable widow? What significant impact could they have?

Well, years later, that little boy became a visionary young man who was determined to do the work of Christ. That little girl became an optimistic young woman of faith. They met at a Christian youth camp, got married, heard the Lord's calling to ministry, and dedicated themselves to serve Him in reaching India for Christ. They both came to Christ because someone who was living beyond himself brought them into the orbit of the Gospel. And now they have become fully committed to living beyond themselves, too.

Today, I know them as the co-founders of Mission India — the couple that John DeVries first partnered with more than 40 years ago. They are the visionary leaders upon whose shoulders the entire mission and ministry of Mission India was built.

What happens when you live beyond yourself? Since then, this couple has developed outreach programs that have brought the Gospel into the lives of more than 77 million children, like Monika and Bishal. Their inspirational leadership has energized tens of thousands of workers from more than 1,500 Indian denominations to plant tens of thousands of new churches in every state of India. Over 1.5 million illiterate men and women have learned to read, thanks to their leadership. Thousands of villages, including Karsenbai's village, have been transformed. At least 20 million people have claimed to profess Christ as an outcome of their ministries. And their impact today continues to grow and expand at an even faster pace. Talk about living beyond yourself! Without a hint of hyperbole, I can say I know of no other people who have equaled the impact on the Kingdom of God in my lifetime.

Who could have imagined that God would choose to use these two humble servants to make His name known all over India? The widespread impact of their faithfulness continues to stagger our comprehension.

So, we will continue to plan, to pray, to dream, to measure outcomes, and to declare the praises of the one who empowers our ministries. And we will continue to trust God to do "immeasurably more" than we can even imagine.

Because, when we live beyond ourselves, we know He will.

Questions for discussion:

1. Read again Ephesians 3:18-20. In your opinion, which of the stories told in this chapter best illustrates the truth of that passage?

2. Have you ever experienced an answer to prayer that was far beyond your expectations?

3. Are you waiting for an answer to prayer that is "greater than you could imagine"? How might you pray differently if that were your expectation?

CHAPTER 14:
Entering the Kingdom

Imagine going to Disneyland. You get your admittance ticket and you stand in the entrance. The entrance itself is beautiful. You see the landscape and buildings and rides in the distance. There's a bit of a "wow" factor. You've got Aladdin, Buzz Lightyear, and Mickey walking around!

But what if – every time you went to Disneyland – you simply stood at the entrance and never went inside? The "wow" factor would still be there, but your passion would soon fade.

Then, imagine someone coming up to you and saying, "Follow me!" That person takes you by the hand, walks you through the entrance, and suddenly you're inside. There are rides and thrills and excitement. Then, you realize how close you've always been to this magical kingdom — just steps away — but never enjoyed it.

You see where I'm going with this, don't you? A lot of us live our lives like that. We miss the power of Kingdom living because we make the Gospel about ourselves and about getting into Heaven. We think the Kingdom is something in the far future, and, therefore, we don't really enter in and enjoy it now. We miss the joy of Kingdom living that is available to us today. We can experience this joy when we intentionally help people discover the love of Christ. That's what it means to enter the Kingdom. Jesus said, "Your father has been pleased to give you the kingdom. Sell your possessions and give to the poor..." (Luke 12:32-33). The Kingdom of God exists for us wherever and whenever we live as if Jesus is on the throne! When we play a part in people receiving Jesus as their Savior, we are not only bringing them into the Kingdom of God, we are also entering into the joy of the Kingdom ourselves. Otherwise, we are just standing at the gates and looking in.

Yet it can be tempting for us to pass the buck, to make excuses. "So-and-so would be more effective than me." "I don't have any training or experience." "I don't feel qualified." Or even, "It's not my spiritual gift."

Well, consider this story from the first chapter of Exodus:

> The king of Egypt said to the Hebrew midwives, whose names were Shiphrah and Puah, "When you are helping the Hebrew women during childbirth on the delivery stool, if you see that the baby is a boy, kill him; but if it is a girl, let her live." The midwives, however, feared God and did not do what the king of Egypt had told them to do; they let the boys live. Then the king of Egypt summoned the midwives and asked them, "Why have you done this? Why have

you let the boys live?" The midwives answered Pharaoh, "Hebrew women are not like Egyptian women; they are vigorous and give birth before the midwives arrive." So God was kind to the midwives and the people increased and became even more numerous (vv. 15-20).

When we read Exodus, we can see so many parallels between the story of Exodus and the story of our world today.

There are always some people who live for God, who know the fear of the Lord, just like Puah and Shiphrah of Exodus 1:15-20. I love the story of these two women. These midwives enjoyed an intimate network of contacts with the families of Israel. They knew what was going on, and they were tough.

I'm not a mom. But I'm smart enough to know childbirth is not easy. These midwives had seen it all and experienced so many difficulties of life. They were now being ordered to add a tragic burden to the pain of childbirth. They refused to do it. So, let's be honest and admit that these women lie. They tell their lies out of reverence to God, and at the risk of their own lives. I think the Bible shares these details with us for a reason. First of all, they let us know that God uses imperfect people. If God can use two lying midwives, He can use me.

There is also a bigger reason why we are told about the courage of Shiphrah and Puah: God uses ordinary people to advance His Kingdom.

"The midwives, however, feared God and did not do what the king of Egypt had told them to do" (Exodus 1:17).

When we think about the Exodus story, it's easy to assume that it begins with the story of Moses. But it doesn't. It begins with two ordinary, flawed women who step forward to defy a king. We know their names. What is the name of the king? We are not even told his name. He has disappeared from the pages of history; but the names of Shiphrah and Puah are preserved forever in God's book.

In the hierarchy of Egypt, the Pharaoh is on top, and the midwives are at the very bottom. God wanted the names of Shiphrah and Puah to go in His book. He wanted those names remembered. And today, more than 3,400 years later, we can still talk about them and admire them.

It's still happening today. God is preserving in His book the names of the ordinary people who are carrying out His will. Mission India seeks to honor, support, and empower those people in every way that we can. There was a time when a few foreign missionaries laid the foundation for God's work in India. That day has passed. God's work there, as in so many places around the world, is now carried on by local people, people who know the cultures and languages of their communities, and who have the networks of contacts, just like those midwives in Egypt. Those same ordinary people in India are able to confront authorities and rulers who are trying to stop God's work. And

God performs miracles through them.

Jesus followed the same principle during His life on earth. He recruited ordinary people, trained and inspired them, and entrusted them with God's agenda for reaching the world with the Gospel. They witnessed, they saw people come to Christ, they planted churches, and they did it all without academic degrees. But they had courage and commitment.

In Acts 1, there were just a few believers. In Acts 2, 3,000 became believers. A few chapters later, we read that over 5,000 had come into the churches. By AD 100, the churches are believed to have multiplied and grown to 25,000. And by AD 350, perhaps to more than 30 million. The vast majority of the first Christians were slaves or from the lowest levels of society. But the Gospel eventually saturated and captured the people of the Roman Empire at all levels of society.

This was no surprise. Jesus promised, "...on this rock I will build my church, and the gates of Hades will not overcome it" (Matthew 16:18). He is still fulfilling that promise. In a typical year, Mission India trains and equips several thousand Church Planters who plant thousands of reproducing churches each year. Churches are also planted through Adult Literacy Classes and Children's Bible Clubs. I like to think of them as "rabbit churches" – much smaller, harder to see, and reproducing like crazy. They don't draw a lot of attention, which is important considering all of the persecution taking place.

All of this makes for a great harvest for the Kingdom. God has already raised up workers for this harvest, and – like the midwives of Exodus 1 – these workers are doing the will of God.

I love that in Exodus 1:20 it says, "…and the people increased and became even more numerous." God loves to multiply the agents doing His work. We see this happening all over India today. Nothing deters them. Luke 10:2 says, "Ask the Lord of the harvest, therefore, to send out workers into his harvest field." Yet, Indian leaders say God has already answered this prayer; He has raised up thousands of willing workers. They are so eager to reach their countrymen. But they don't know what to do or how to do it. They are desperate for training and resources, and they are praying for partners who can help them.

Such was the case with Divij.

Divij was one of nine children born into a poor family in a village on the east coast of India. When he was sixteen years old, he heard the Good News from a friend and made a decision to follow Christ. Divij testifies, "Two years after becoming a Christian, while I was praying, I received a clear and miraculous vision from Jesus to go to southern India and bring the Gospel to the people there." The very next morning, Divij went to the railway station and took the next train going south. He went as far as the ticket he could afford would take him. For the next two months, he slept on a railway platform. He had no money, no training, no friends, and no supporters, just a lot of passion to obey the heavenly vision.

He looked around the city and saw street children everywhere. Instead of being in school, they were begging or stealing. And they presented Divij with his first evangelistic challenge. He told them Bible stories. He prayed for healing for many of them. For two years, he lived the life of a homeless person. One day, he prayed for a little girl, the only daughter of a widow. The girl was healed, and the widow took Divij in as a tenant.

For ten years, Divij did his best. He witnessed to hundreds of people. On three occasions, he was beaten by thugs who opposed his ministry. Once he was jailed. Without financial support, he was always hungry. But he kept on going. By 1987, he had led ten people to Jesus and was leading them in worship every Sunday. A pastor in another church told him about our Church Planter Training program in a nearby city. Divij applied and was accepted into the program.

People like Divij have this unquenchable thirst to tell everyone about Jesus, to gather new believers, to pray in Jesus' name for the needs of the people around them. They hand out Christian literature; they write Bible verses on boulders; they preach to crowds in marketplaces; they lay their hands on the sick and pray for healing. Most of them don't know how to start a worshipping group, disciple a new believer, organize a church, survive in a hostile environment, raise up elders, or even organize a Sunday school class. They are just not familiar with all of the actions needed to build a healthy church.

In the meantime, they might face opposition, even physical attack, by local Hindus extremists. They often go without food or live in one-room shacks. Their families suffer, high-caste neighbors despise them, and often the established, mainline churches ignore or shun them. Still, they have heard the call. They don't give up. They look for help wherever they can find it.

When Divij began his training in 1987 he learned the skills and discipline to do even more for God. During his first year of training, he established ten prayer groups, helped one hundred people find Jesus Christ, and baptized forty of them. But Divij's most dramatic impact began when he recruited others to join his team. Today, Divij has trained 108 evangelists, ordinary people who have established prayer groups in two hundred villages. After more than thirty years, he and his disciples have started 185 churches, 35 with their own buildings. One church started at a Christian high school with 500 students and 15 staff. His original church, not far from the railway platform on which he once slept, now has 1,100 members. The walls of the sanctuary are covered with banners and posters detailing the church's goals and objectives. Divij is still passionate and has big goals to reach tens of thousands more people with the Gospel.

God has already raised up thousands of people like Divij all over India, even in the Hindu heartlands of the north and among Muslim-majority populations. God is shouting to us, "Come and see where my Holy Spirit is working! Come and join in reaping a great harvest!"

There is no greater place to do that than in India. I have communicated this throughout this entire book. Because of that reality, it would be wrong of me *not* to ask you to join with the people you have met throughout this book to advance God's Kingdom in India.

Asking yourself where you begin is the most practical first step to this challenge. My answer is two-fold: Pray and understand that it simply begins with believing that God wants to use you. The Bible says very clearly, "But you are the ones chosen by God, chosen for the high calling of priestly work, chosen to be a holy people, God's instruments to do his work and speak out for him, to tell others of the night-and-day difference he made for you…" 1 Peter 2:9 (MSG).

When Peter wrote that, he wasn't speaking at a pastors' conference. He was writing to ordinary people like you and me. But there was a problem with their thinking. In the Old Testament, before Jesus took on human flesh, God's Spirit worked through a select group of people called "priests." These Old Testament priests served as mediators between God and His people. The average Israelite didn't have a direct line to God, so he had to be represented by a priest. But when Jesus came into the world, He turned the religious culture upside down as He started identifying normal, everyday people as priests. He would look at crowds and say things like, "You! Yes, I'm talking to you. You are the light of the world." "You! Yes, all of you … will be my witnesses…"

Then one day, a day called the Day of Pentecost, a group of those non-priestly, ordinary people, who had walked with Jesus after He had risen from the dead, huddled together to pray in an upper room. God's Holy Spirit settled on everybody's head — not just a select few. The message was clear: Everyone who follows Jesus Christ has direct access to God. Everyone who follows Christ has the supernatural power of the Holy Spirit. Everyone has been anointed as a priest to carry God's love and hope to a lost and broken world so loved by God. That includes you and me. But it all begins with believing that God's Spirit lives in us and wants to use us to live beyond ourselves. We just need to start by asking God, "How do you want to use me?"

One of my favorite Bible stories is the story of God calling Moses to set the captives free. In one of the many conversations that God and Moses have, Moses is telling God why he is unusable. God asks Moses, "What is that in your hand?" (Exodus 4:2). When Moses answers by telling God he has a rod in his hand, God says, "Throw it on the ground" (v. 3). Moses obeys, and God transforms what Moses had into a living organism.

I think that God's question to Moses is one we should all consider. The rod that Moses carried represented who he was. He was a shepherd; the rod represented his identity, his influence, and his place in society. God was encouraging Moses to give it to Him, and He would transform it to bring life. I want to challenge you to think about what's in your hand. Will you lay it down and allow God to use it and transform it to impact others way beyond yourself?

When I first went to India, John DeVries invited me because of what I had in my hand. I was a pastor who had spiritual influence over people. When I returned, I knew God wanted me to use that influence for the advancement of the Great Commission in India. One Sunday, I told a story about a remote church I had visited in India. The offering was being taken there and I saw a woman bring a bag of rice to the offering. I asked a Mission India partner about this and he told me that some people are so poor that the only thing they have to give to the church is rice from their own table. He shared that every night before they cook the rice, they put a handful in a bag and take it to church as their offering. After I shared this story with the church I was pastoring, I passed out rice bags and asked people to fill them with change or whatever it was that God placed in their hand and to give it toward advancing the Kingdom of God in India. The next Sunday, people brought little rice bags filled with resources that God had placed in their hands. Together, our church was able to send nearly 35,000 kids to a Children's Bible Club.

I personally did not have a lot of resources, but I had a church full of people that loved me and trusted me, and I took a risk and asked them to be a part of what God is doing in India. And they said yes. In fact, as I write this, that church is still saying yes to India, over fifteen years later.

I don't know what it is specifically for you. But I do know the Spirit lives in all of us and empowers all of us to live beyond ourselves.

Who knows what God wants to do through you? Maybe, like Saul of Bhopal, it is ministering to a family that has a child who is deathly ill. Maybe, like Monika, God wants to use you to bring your dad into a relationship with Christ. Maybe you are one of the 37 percent that George Barna identifies as knowing and living out the Great Commission. Maybe God wants to use you as an ambassador right in your church to engage the entire church in God's call as it is stated in Matthew 28:18-20. Maybe, like Raju Joseph, God wants to use you to speak for those who are so marginalized that they cannot speak for themselves. Maybe you need to pray the B.L.E.S.S. Prayer over five people for five minutes every day.

The promise is that, just like Puah and Shiphrah who chose to live beyond themselves and took those steps of faith to bring life into this world, you will be a part of the heroes of faith, the countless people who used what God gave them for His glory so that He would do immeasurably more than they could ever ask or imagine.

My hope is that, as you have read this book, you have a sense of urgency to see people come to know Jesus. The problem is that if we miss this opportunity, millions of people will live their lives and end up in Hell apart from Jesus and His love.

Paul says in Philippians 1:6, "...being confident of this, that he who began a good work in you will carry it on to completion until the day of Christ Jesus." God promises that He is going to finish what He has started through individuals and our witness to the Gospel. We are all invited to demonstrate and declare the love of God.

In Esther 4:14, Mordecai is pleading with Esther to step into the call of God, but she is hesitant. Mordecai then says to her, "For if you remain silent at this time, relief and deliverance for the Jews will arise from another place..." What he is saying to her is that this is going to happen with or without you. The question is: Do we want to be in on what God is doing?

It is my prayer that we all understand this question as we look at the world. God's vision of redemption is so big, we simply cannot do it alone. We all need to live beyond ourselves and step into this calling. The nation of India alone is 1.3 billion strong, worshipping 330 million gods and goddesses. We are engaged in a spiritual battle with the forces of evil. We need intercessors, advocates, and financial partners aligned with the Good News of the Gospel.

We do this so God can receive glory among the nations, so the nations can experience the peace and power of the Kingdom of God. We, as believers, experience the blessing of being obedient in living out the Great Commission and we experience the surpassing joy of seeing people, families, villages, cities, and nations transformed by the love of Christ.

Will you join me in using all God has given you to live beyond yourself?

Questions for discussion:

1. How do the stories in this chapter illustrate the importance of living beyond ourselves?

2. What might God be calling you to when it comes to living beyond yourself for India?

Sources

1. Keller, Timothy. *Counterfeit Gods: The Empty Promises of Money, Sex, and Power, and the Only Hope that Matters*. New York: Penguin Books, 2016.

2. Shaw, Joey. *All Authority: How the Authority of Christ Upholds the Great Commission*. Nashville: B&H Publishing Group, 2016.

3. Weber, Jeremy. "Incredible Indian Christianity: A Special Report on the World's Most Vibrant Christward Movement." *Christianity Today*. Oct. 2016. https://www.christianitytoday.com/ct/2016/november/incredible-india-christianity-special-report-christward-mov.html

4. Barna Group. *Transforming the Great Commission*. Carol Stream: Tyndale House Publishers, Inc., 2018.

5. Bosch, David. *Transforming Mission, Paradigm Shifts in Theology of Mission*. Maryknoll: Orbis Books, 2011.

6. Kung, Hans. *On Being a Christian*. New York: Doubleday, 1976.

7. *Los Angeles Times*. East Bay Times, 2005, https://www.eastbaytimes.com/2005/06/04/s-f-hospital-part-of-study-on-power-of-prayer/

8. Creasy Dean, Kendra. *Almost Christian: What the Faith of Our Teenagers is Telling the American Church*. New York: Oxford University Press, Inc., 2010.

9. Packer, J. I. *Knowing God*. Westmont: InterVarsity Press, 1993.

10. Chapman, Gary. *The Five Love Languages*. Chicago: Northfield Publishing, 1995.

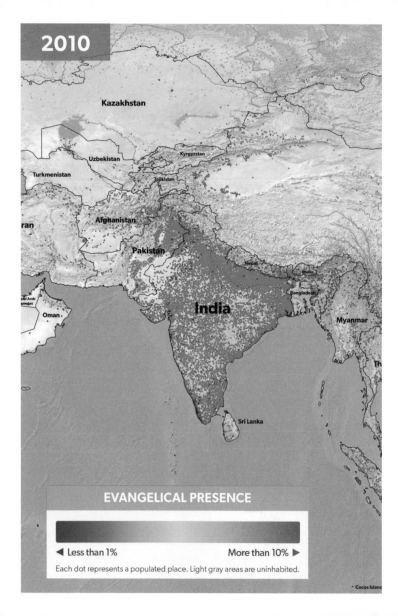

2010

Kazakhstan

Uzbekistan

Kyrgyzstan

Turkmenistan

Tajikistan

Iran

Afghanistan

Pakistan

Nepal

Bhutan

Bangladesh

India

Myanmar

United Arab Emirates

Oman

Sri Lanka

Th

EVANGELICAL PRESENCE

◀ Less than 1%   More than 10% ▶

Each dot represents a populated place. Light gray areas are uninhabited.

* Cocos Island

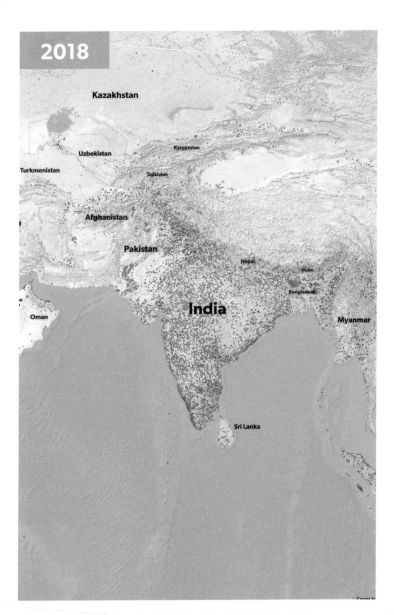